THE PROCESS

OF THE

PROMISE:

Discovering your ultimate life of
Purpose, Passion, Power, Prosperity and Peace

Byron Ravnell

In Memory of D.T.

"Man if you had been here, I would have finished this thing 3 or 4 years ago..."

CONTENTS

ACKNOWLEDGMENTS

Thanks to…

My two Issac(s) Langston and Bryson: You are Princes of the Promise- my great name and nation. I speak that God blesses each of you… in every place you go… in everything you do… every day of your life!!

Penny, you are truly a woman that seeks the heart of God. Thank you for all you have shown me. Hold on to the fire!!

Mama Pie, thank you for "living" your Christianity and being a fine example…even if you didn't bake me cookies.

Melvalyn, Aneita, Gerry and my entire family-- thanks for walking with me all of these years.

Ron "Starr" Wills, Chris "Kristofferson" Jones, "Nacky", Paul, Eddie and each person that shared "good or bad" theology during long conversations over the years-- I'm sure there are bits and pieces of you throughout the book.

D. Banks, thanks for the opportunity to return to my first love of radio and allowing me to share spiritual wisdom with your listeners-Man, there ain't nothing wrong with a little funk- God don't mind!!!!

Thanks to Charles and Cassandra Moore, Bud and Clauda Orrell, Dennis & RR Chapel, Joe Bedford and Toliver's Chapel; all of whom gave me an opportunity to exercise my gift.

Thanks to everyone who assisted in the production of this book, Jacob- you are truly DA' MAN!! Also, Yamina, Bethany and LaTonya "T.T." Lynch.

Special thanks to my Sweet Home Family, a people with warm loving hearts-- THANK YOU for providing a venue for my voice, and your ears to hear as God spoke to me about his great and many Promises… I thank God for each of you!!!

…And finally, to each person that reads this book…May you believe wholeheartedly, anticipate daily, seek without fear and realize fully all of God's Promises!

INTRODUCTION

Welcome to *The Process of The Promise*. This book is about living a great life. But not just a great life—the life that you were designed to live.

This book is about finding your unique path, making it through the maze of confusing events and disheartening episodes that life throws at you. This is a book about realizing your God-given potential simply by understanding and receiving your God-given promises.

Through an imaginary show of hands, how many of you know that you have a calling from deep within that says you have a place to be and a mission to fulfill—yet you know that you are doing neither?

Or perhaps you have an idea of what it is that you have been placed upon this revolving chunk of dirt called Earth to do—but you just don't know how to start or how to navigate the course. Maybe you're one of the many that have no idea what it is you have been called to do, but you know for sure that what you're doing right now isn't it. Well, this book is written just for you!

First and foremost in the process, each person has to understand that who they are—their physical, mental, spiritual, physiological, and emotional makeup—didn't just happen by accident. It was actually planned before the beginning of time.

Just as amazing, the overall plot of our lives - and the countless "subplots" within that overall plot, all particular components of your Promise, were designed and set in motion at the same time—in the beginning. All of those plots, major and minor, then influence the decisions each of us make, as well as external forces beyond our control.

The path, needless to say, can be full of surprises, discouragement, and even seem impossible at times; but, be assured, there is, if not a final ending point, a desired and definite place that holds that which will provide a sense of fulfillment that no other place in your life can.

If you are excited, maybe even a bit anxious to find out more about this life-fulfilling calling, I don't blame you. This is a longing that has been instilled in each and every one of us since before time, modeled in the promise that God gave to Abraham in the Old Testament. This promise, which is corporate or general in nature, has been passed along to us through generations as a covenant from God; but in addition, we all, each of us, have individual promises to discover in our own lives.

Throughout the course of this book, you will walk through each step of discovering God's promises to you both on a larger scale and on an individual basis. You will be made aware of signposts and landmarks that will assist you in keeping your bearings along the way. You will learn that your journey, although personal to you and personalized specifically for you, is similar to the journeys undertaken by many men and women that have made special contributions to the world simply because they began and—just as importantly—continued down the path to their destiny.

As you may have learned by now, discovering your promise isn't always easy, but it is the most rewarding life journey that you will ever take. *The Process of The Promise* is essential to living a fulfilling life, and its also inescapable.

I am excited to begin your journey with you as you pursue God's promise and learn to live a life of purpose, passion, power, peace and prosperity!

Let's begin…

1

THE PROCESS OF THE PROMISE

(Genesis 12:1-3) **Now the LORD said to Abram, "Go from your country and your kindred and your father's house to the land that I will show you. I will make of you a great nation, and I will bless you, and make your name great, so that you will be a blessing. I will bless those who bless you, and the one who curses you I will curse; and in you all the families of the earth shall be blessed."** (NRSV)

Process- noun \ˈprä-ˌses, ˈprō-, -səs\ a : PROGRESS, ADVANCE <in the process of time> (1) : a natural phenomenon marked by gradual changes that lead toward a particular result <the process of growth>

Example: Few good things in life are gained overnight, but rather through a life-long process.

Promise- noun \ˈprä-məs\ a : a declaration that one will do or refrain from doing something specified b : a legally binding declaration that gives the person to whom it is made a right to expect or to claim the performance …of a specified act 2 : reason to expect something; especially : ground for expectation of success, improvement, or excellence 3: something that is promised

Example: God never made a promise that he didn't intend to keep.

From: Merriam Webster Collegiate Dictionary
http://www.merriam-webster.com/dictionary/process

S imply put, it all began with a promise—one promise from God to man. The destiny of an entire people, that would shape the course of the world for generations to come—all came from just one word, given to one person from God. Actually, when you think about it, all things great and small have begun with just that, one God-inspired word, thought, or dream spoken into the heart of one man or woman, new ideas that changed previously held views, new technology that led to new industry, new forms of government that led to new nations. All these things came from one thought, idea, dream, or promise, placed into the heart and head of mankind.

Even more amazing is that the recipients of the promises were just ordinary people like you and me. The only difference is they discerned the word of promise for their life, believed what God said, and chose to act upon it, and continued to act in faith until the promise was fulfilled.

God has made promises to each and every one of us through His Word, the Bible. The most important points to remember about God's promises are that they are for our good, and they impact every area of our lives. Secondly, we must remember that promises are nothing more than seeds of future potential, and all seeds require a period of time and suitable care to transition into what it is intended to be. No person, plant, or thing began its existence fully formed; each required time and care for formation, development, conditioning, transitioning, and success.

If you have ever found yourself struggling to live out God's promises of peace, prosperity, health, and happiness, there may be one key factor that you have overlooked in your journey.

God's Promises Require a Process

We all have the potential to access every one of God's promises—but you must be willing to undertake a life-long journey to get there.

4

To begin, let me give you the definition of the Promise as it pertains to our life of purpose.

Promise: God's desire for us, and the agreement with us to direct us to our greater purpose and to help us complete that particular task.

These promises are made to each of us, and the Bible is full of examples of God's promises to His people throughout history.

Some of the first and best examples of God's promises are to Abraham in Genesis, where he is promised a new land, a nation of descendants, and unlimited blessings from God for him and his family throughout time (Genesis 12: 2-3). Since we are all descendants of Abraham through the blood of Christ, these promises and blessings apply directly to you today.

(Galatians 3:29) **And if ye be Christ's, then are ye Abraham's seed, and heirs according to the promise.**

This is excellent news if you have felt defeated, depressed, beaten-down, and like you aren't getting the most out of your life. We have all been there, and we have all felt unfulfilled at times. Yet, because we are the descendants of Abraham, we too can expect God's protection and blessings. We have a great hope before us as we begin our journey to pursue our promises and full potential promised to us by God.

Because the journey to the Promise is long and full of learning experiences, it could be termed the Process of the Promise. This process has an intended outcome based upon the plan and purpose that God has ordained specifically for you. As you can probably gather, the Process takes time and is the path that we travel throughout life to receive all that God has in store for each of us.

But there's more! In addition to the above examples that are general promises made to each of us throughout the Bible, God also has unique and specific promises that He has made for your life and no one else's. These particular promises are given to each person based upon their specific destiny.

So how do you access these promises from God that are both general and specific to your life's purpose? We can find the answer in Romans:

(Romans 4:13) **It was not through law that Abraham and his offspring received the promise that he would be heir of the world, but through the righteousness that comes by faith.**

(Romans 4:16) **Therefore, the promise comes by faith, so that it may be by grace and may be guaranteed to all Abraham's offspring-- not only to those who are of the law but also to those who are of the faith of Abraham. He is the father of us all.**

For us to access the promise and find our unique purpose, given to us by God Himself, we must follow His guidance, in faith, casting all fear aside. While this often seems "easier said than done," it also helps to consider that Abraham found himself in similar circumstances as those we experience today. Setting aside the obvious differences of the time period (several thousand years ago) and some of the details, the hardships, trials, discouragements and even the triumphs Abraham experienced on his journey toward his promises from God are very similar to those experienced by people today.

Yes, Abraham was given big promises from God about becoming a great nation of blessed people, but how did he know that it was really going to happen? Abraham had to deal with the same fear, anxiety, and challenges that we all do today as he followed God to reach his own promises by faith.

Along this path, don't expect to walk perfectly because you will encounter your share of challenges; perfection is impossible. You can expect to make mistakes as you come upon obstacles in your journey, yet that is why God's grace is there, to guide you and cushion your fall. God has promised to be with us each step of the way, so rest assured that life's hurdles are all part of the process to receive your promises.

The good news is, just as you can expect hurdles along the path of the promise, you can also expect blessings upon blessings as you follow the path that God desires for you. Challenges are a part of the process that leads you to the product, which are the blessings that result from the promise. For greater clarity:

Process—the procedure, course or method by which we obtain God's promises.

Product—That for which we strive; the results; what God has promised.

The process is your journey along the way, the things you must go through. The product is your destination, what you must get to. In yet another way, the process is the temporary journey that must be endured to receive the product, which are God's permanent blessings.

For a more practical example of the difference between the process and the promise, let's use the analogy of a contestant that competes in a race. The process is the actual race; the sweat, the pain, and the hardships endured to run the race. The conditions and the challenges are real but only last as long as the race—but when the finish line is crossed, all of the pain and hardships are a mere memory, but the product is the prize that you receive upon completion. To go even further, it's not just the trophy for winning, it's the self-gratification and inspiration you receive for being there and competing. The very fact that you won cannot be changed. No matter who wins the next race, you won this one. That fact, the result or product, can't be changed.

What is the product or blessings that you can expect in pursuit of God's promise? I'm glad you asked!

Purpose
Passion
Power
Prosperity
Peace

To understand what it is that God has in store for us, let's look at each of these benefits more closely. Purpose is an interesting concept because it is a noun as well as a verb, an object as well as an action. Purpose is not only what we aim for or hope to attain (noun), it is also what we do to attain that result (verb). In other words, our purpose should suggest consistency in whom and what we are to be, as well as how we act and what we do to be that person. Our actions, what we do, should always line up with and be consistent with our purpose, what God has called us to do and be.

Passion, unfortunately, is an element that is absent from so many lives today, and the result of that absence can be seen in the faces of the multitudes that wander aimlessly through empty, mundane lives. Passion results in anticipation and conviction to begin and continue the process of our promise. Passion will provide the conviction to begin when reason says no, and will sustain you when circumstances say to quit. A purpose without passion is similar to a battery operated light that doesn't burn brightly; even though it was designed to illuminate the way and has the capacity to do so, the light will only shine as bright as the source that powers it. A weak battery provides a light that is sub-par and less than what the creator of that light intended. Any idea given by God, but not implemented with the desire and intensity of passion, will never fully bless the world as it was intended, and will never honor the Lord that ordained it. Passion ensures that your purpose will not die a premature death or grow old without it reaching its full potential.

Power, though often given a bad name by those who don't truly understand it, is an essential and guaranteed element of any God-given promise. Defined as simply as possible, power is influence. When you think about it, it should go without saying that power is guaranteed with any promise. Otherwise, how could God expect you to accomplish that for which you were designed, without the power or influence to get it done? 2 Timothy 1:7 confirms this: **"For God hath not given us the spirit of fear; but of power, and of love, and of a sound mind."**(KJV)

Prosperity is the most misunderstood concept on this list of blessings. Most anyone today, when asked to define prosperity would say money or riches. While I'll agree that prosperity does have much to do with finances, to view prosperity as money or financial wealth alone reveals a lack of depth and understanding of what a life of promise truly is. True prosperity is multifaceted and multilayered; it is not just one thing. True prosperity is a combination of all of the blessings above, a true package deal. Prosperity is having something to live for (purpose), that you are willing to die for (passion), that you were prepared and equipped for (power), that regardless of all the ups and downs and ins and outs, you remain confident that this is what you were created to do (peace). Yes, prosperity does not mean just being rich in money, but it means being rich in all areas of your life.

Peace should be the most desired product of the promise, without it, the enjoyment of all the other products is minimized, if not absent. It is peace that allows us to be fully present and appreciate what the promise has provided. Without peace, a person may sleep for hours on end, but never find rest, or live in a mansion that is nothing more than a grand prison of emptiness and pain. It is peace that allows one to truly enjoy the pleasures that God's promises offer. I have met many poor people that were rich because of the peace that abounded in their life, while conversely, I've met many wealthy people who possessed many desirable trinkets, toys, and possessions, but their life, although filled with stuff, was empty and cold. Of all the blessings that the promise offers, peace is the grand prize.

These blessings are the Product of the Promise.

If the *promise* is what God desires of us, then it is safe to say that the *blessings* are what God desires for us. Because God desires us to have them, you can expect to receive each of these blessings and more as you walk out the journey in the process to pursuing God's promises for your lives.

However, receiving the blessings is not the end of the process. Remember what God said to Abraham:

(Gen. 12:3) **"... and in thee shall all families of the earth be blessed."** (KJV)

Throughout this process, we can expect to receive multiple blessings based on what God desires to give us from His heart, but in order for the process to be complete, there is one more step: we must bless others by sharing all that God has given to us and placed within us from birth. Later in this book, we will look at how the promise, though given to Abraham, was not just for Abraham. For us to be blessed by God and truly fulfill His purpose here on earth, we are to be like Abraham and be a blessing "to all the families of the earth."

If you have longed to find your purpose in life, the path lies right in front of you. As we follow God's guidance and move forward in faith, we enter the process to receive His promises to us.

The fact that God has given us these promises as a people and for our individual lives implies that He has prepared each of us for a unique purpose.

To break it down for you even further:

God has a master plan, and we are all players.

God has prepared each of us, placing within us all the gifts necessary to fulfill our purpose.

These gifts are the means by which God blesses us, and we in turn bless others.

In this simple chain of events, it is clear to see that God's promise is the fulfillment of the unique purpose He has for each of us here on earth. We access God's promise through the process and journey along the way, where we receive abundant blessings and are then able to bless those around us.

As you can see, this is a very exciting reality for God's people! Not only do we have concrete promises passed down from Abraham, but we each have our own unique life plan full of promises and blessings to uncover along the way.

When we are able to view God's purpose for our lives in light of His tender and loving heart, it is a truly beautiful thing. God has created a unique purpose for you that is all your own. This is the final destination that will offer you the life of fulfillment, happiness, peace, and stability that you deserve. However, to get there, we must be willing to embrace the Process, which I will discuss throughout this book. Along this journey, we can expect to be showered with blessings from God, that will in turn bless those in our lives, yet the clear end in sight is our life purpose promised to us by God.

From the following verse, here are a few important facts to remember about God's promises to you:

(John 10:10) **"...I am come that they might have life and that they might have it more abundantly."**

First, all of God's promises are present in your life, and they are for good. Before any person can access a life of abundance, he or she must decide one fundamental truth in their approach to life and the promises of God: whether they will view the universe as a friend or foe. In other words, are the blessings of God for you, or just for everyone else? Many people walk through life with constant fears and expectations for the worst, and the worst is what they get. There are many names given to this universal law such as the law of attraction. The biblical law is stated in Proverbs 23:7: **"as a man thinketh so is he,"** or, what you believe is what you receive.

Fully understanding the abundant stores of promises that God has for you will lift a burden off of your shoulders and show you that someone is on your side.

God reaffirms his desires for our success many times in scripture:

(Jeremiah 29:11) (NIV) **"'For I know the plans I have for you,' declares the LORD, 'plans to prosper you and not to harm you, plans to give you hope and a future.'"**

(3Jo 1:2) **"Beloved, I wish above all things that thou mayest prosper and be in health, even as thy soul prospereth."**

It can't get any clearer than that! God has sought, and continually seeks ways to bless us; He is for us and not against us. Understanding this foundational truth will make it much easier to access what God has in store for you as you travel the path to your promises.

Second, not only are his promises for good, they are far greater than we can know.

(John 10:10 KJV) **"I am come that they might have life and that they might have it more abundantly."**

Christ, when describing his mission here on earth, states that his reason for being is that *we* may have life, and a life that is more abundant. Jesus used the word abundant, which means "marked by great supply" to impress upon us that his blessings are not scarce or limited. If Christ came to bless us abundantly, and his supply is not limited, then the question becomes: why do we limit what we receive with low expectations? Why do so many of us settle for an appetizer when God has invited us to His generous buffet? To live lives of the promise, we must challenge flawed mindsets, expect and move toward abundant blessings, then reach out and grab all that God offers.

In a very interesting survey conducted by The Barna Group in 2008, different groups of Christians were asked what they wanted most out of life. Surprisingly, the survey revealed 19 different possible life purpose outcomes. Some of the results varied according to personal beliefs and spiritual commitments within a diverse group of Christians, as well as agnostics and atheists.

The results showed that evangelical Christians, making up 8% of the population, were the only Christian group where 90% listed up to 6 of the 19 life purpose possibilities as "very desirable". These life purpose possibilities included having good health, having a close relationship with God, having a life purpose, living with integrity, having one marital partner for life and a lifelong commitment to the Christian faith. Evangelicals were also the only group where 9 out of 10 people answered that a clear life purpose, good health, and good integrity were their top goals.

This Christian group seems to have the right idea about pursuing their purpose in life. However, this group only listed a maximum of 6 out of 19 life purpose possibilities as their top desires, which is actually quite a low score when you put it in perspective.

Why did these Christians only ask for 6? Why not all 19? This is what so many Christians do—set the bar too low and dream too small. In reality, there are bountiful promises that God wants to give to all of us if we are only willing.

When Jesus, the Light and Savior of the world, talked about abundant life in John 10:10, it was clear that He did not intend for us to have an average life here on Earth. Not only did Jesus want things to go well, but he wanted them to go better than well—living abundantly above our highest expectations!

As it says in Ephesians 3:20 (NASB), **"Now to Him who is able to do exceeding abundantly beyond all that we ask or think, according to the power that works within us…"** According to this verse, even when we ask God to bless us based on our highest expectations, He still gives us far above anything—anything—that we can ask or even think. This should encourage each of us to ask God for our deepest desires and dreams and expect to be met with even more abundance as He answers your prayers. Dream big in the blessings God has for you!

These truths about God's promises should create a source of great anticipation and expectation in your life.

Instead of keeping your expectations low and living a life devoid of abundance, it is time to walk out your destiny step-by-step as you pursue God's purpose and promises made specifically for you. Only when we are not afraid to be the best we can be, and have all that God desires for us, will we discover our best and most authentic self created by God, designed and equipped to fulfill His purpose for each of us.

In the next chapter, we are going to discuss how the Promise and Purpose God has for our lives are closely related. God's promise to us directs us to our destiny.

For Meditation: How can you distinguish the Promise from the Process? Why are they both important? What does Prosperity mean to you?

(2 Peter 1:3-4) **His divine power has given us everything needed for life and godliness, through the knowledge of him who called us by his own glory and goodness. Thus, he has given us, through these things, his precious and very great promises, so that through them you may escape from the corruption that is in the world because of lust, and may become participants of the divine nature.** (NRSV)

(Psalms 119:160) **All your words are true; all your righteous laws are eternal.** (NIV)

(1 Corinthians 2:9) **But as it is written, Eye hath not seen, nor ear heard, neither have entered into the heart of man, the things which God hath prepared for them that love him.** (KJV)

2

PROMISE IS BASED UPON PURPOSE

(Galatians 3:16) **Now to Abraham and his seed were the promises made.** (KJV)

God's promises are like the stars; the darker the night the brighter they shine. -David Nicholas

If Heaven made him—earth can find some use for him. -Chinese Proverb

The purpose of life is a life of purpose. -Robert Byrne

The promises of God are always indicative of our purpose in life. Your purpose will always be supported by your promises. Never worry about the provision, God has already worked it out... You just focus on doing what you were created to do! -B.R.

Y our Promise is based upon your Purpose, and your Purpose upon your Promise.

An essential component to realizing God's Promise for your life is to understand that your purpose and your promises from God are intricately linked. Your purpose is what you have been designed to do on this earth, and it is synonymous with God's promises for your life.

Our promises from God are directly linked to who we are, encompassing both our past and our future. You may be familiar with the story of Jeremiah in the Bible. Jeremiah was formed by God for a particular purpose, predestined to fulfill his role on this earth.

According to the book of Jeremiah:

(Jeremiah 1:5) **Before I formed you in the womb I knew you, and before you were born I consecrated you; I appointed you a prophet to the nations.** (NRSV)

This verse perfectly captures the personal nature of our creation and continual relationship with God. We understand from this verse that God had knowledge of, and plans for Jeremiah before he was ever conceived in his mother's womb. He was consecrated, chosen, set apart, or made holy. Jeremiah was designed, designated, and destined for the particular purpose of being a prophet to the nations. If you have ever wondered why you are here on this earth, what life is all about, and what your reason for living may be, this verse sums it all up for you. You are not here by accident. You have been created for a purpose. God developed a unique life plan just for you before you were even born.

As amazing as the thought of being designed for a particular purpose may be to you, even more amazing is the realization that, for some of us, that particular purpose may be as specific as being created for one person, place, or particular moment in time. To think that God, according to a "master plan" that was made before time began, consecrated you to be the "solution" for one particular problem in a complicated mass of problems. Perhaps you are familiar with the Bible story of Esther.

Esther was an orphan who was taken in by her relative Mordecai after her parents died. Not only was she an orphan, she was also born to the Jewish people, who were enslaved at this time. Even though the Bible said she was "fair," or beautiful, the circumstances of her early life would be considered dire, to say the least. When the king began the search for a new queen, Esther was chosen as one of the maidens to vie for the position. During her time of preparation, Esther became well liked by the court official over the harem, eventually becoming queen. Not long after, Haman, one of the King's officials devised a plan to kill all of the Jews. When the plan became known by Esther's adoptive father Mordecai, he sent word to her asking that she intervene on behalf of her people. Esther, although queen, was afraid to approach the king because of a rule of that time that those who went before the king without being summoned faced the risk of death, unless the king chose to spare their life. Mordecai, who understood that God often places people in the right place at the right time to do the right thing, sent the following reply to Esther to ensure that she understood that, as well.

(Esther 4:13) **He [Mordecai] sent back this answer: "Do not think that because you are in the king's house you alone of all the Jews will escape.**

(Esther 4:14) **For if you remain silent at this time, relief and deliverance for the Jews will arise from another place, but you and your father's family will perish. And who knows but that you have come to royal position for such a time as this?"** (NIV)

Was it coincidental? Or could it be that Esther, an orphaned slave girl who was blessed with beauty and a wise adoptive father, would also find the favor of those that cared for her? Was it also coincidental that she would then be chosen as queen and then be given favor in the eyes of her polygamous king who chose Esther as a replacement for the former queen who had been killed for failing to follow his instructions? Coincidental? I don't think so.

As you walk the path of promise, and experience the guidance of God over your life, you too will encounter things that will make you ask the question: was that just a coincidence or is there a greater power at work in my life?

How do we know what our purpose in life is?

Many people naturally think that God's purpose for their life is mysterious and difficult to understand. Not so! While there is no cut-and-dry formula for discovering our life purpose, there are some signposts that you can use to navigate your way to God's many promises for you.

Your Dreams

According to Psalms:

(Psalm 37:4) **Take delight in the LORD, and he will give you the desires of your heart.** (NIV)

As you grow closer to God in your personal relationship, you will be able to trust in your natural desires and dreams. God has equipped you with natural desires and passions that directly link to the purpose that He has in store for you.

The process is simple. Put your focus on God, pursue Him in your life, and trust that your natural desires and passions are in line with what God has in store for you. This gives you amazing freedom as you follow God on your journey toward His promises for you. If you have hidden passions or specific talents that light your fire and make you excited about life, it's highly likely that God has given you those gifts as a part of His greater purpose!

As in all endeavors, as you move forward, trusting your natural desires and passions, it is imperative that the "divine operations manual", The Bible, serve as your roadmap and boundary marker. Because our desires can sometimes be based in selfish motives and our actions contrary to what God desires of us, we must verify that our plans and actions fall within the scope of God's acceptable actions. Over the years, I have developed a simple litmus test; before embarking upon any plan or action, ask these questions:

1. What does the Bible say? Is what you are considering in agreement or contradiction to what God said about our actions in his Word?

2. Are you acting out of love? What is the true motivation for what you are doing? Will someone be hurt or adversely affected by your action?

3. Is there glory or shame in what you're doing? If God was present (sometimes we forget he is always present), would you do this thing anyway?

If, after asking these questions, you can still in good conscience do whatever it is you had planned to do, you can rest comfortably that you are on the right track.

Secondly, dreams that are tied to your true purpose are forever present. Although, the call of purpose may be stronger at times than it is at other times, divine dreams and hopes may be eclipsed by the weights and cares of the world, but they can never be ripped from our souls.

To give you a bit of clarity, there is a distinct difference between a dream and a whim. Your life dreams will keep coming back to you again and again, almost tormenting you as you long to pursue them. True dreams are like the sun. Although its' light may be hidden under the cover of darkness or obscured by the clouds on a dreary day, it is forever present and will shine again. The feature that best distinguishes dreams from whims is this: dreams are not conditional or predicated upon external situations. In other words, dreams don't come and go based upon events and circumstances. Whims, however, more often than not, are a temporary solution to a temporary problem; they have nothing to do with God's ultimate purpose for you. A whim is just that - a thought, an idea, or even a temptation that comes across your path that is not in your best long term interest to pursue. Fortunately, you can weigh any whims in your journey against your recurring life dreams to see whether or not they are worth following. Your life dreams will be the ingrained passions God has placed within you that you simply can't shake or let go of.

As an example, imagine you are experiencing financial hardships and read an article that reports one particular occupation is experiencing tremendous growth and high starting salaries. This particular occupation is something that you may have a slight interest in, and could even be a skill that would benefit you in the long run. However, once you take a moment to analyze your thoughts, you realize it is not a career that you had ever considered before reading the article, and the only true reason for considering it is that starting salaries are high in that field, and you need an answer to your current financial problems. Your interest is not in the position but in finding an answer to your financial problems. This is an example of a whim. Contrarily, true dreams are not based upon filling a short-term need, but truly about fulfilling a long term void.

Pursuing God's purpose for our lives is not always as complicated as we make it out to be.

Many people get "performance anxiety" as they pursue God's promises for their lives. What if I make the wrong choice? What if I do something wrong? What if I never find God's purpose for my life?

To get past the anxiety and on the road to the promise, start by throwing all of that anxiety out the window. The truth is that a ship can't be directed if it is still at the dock. Instead of worrying about every single small decision that you make in pursuing God's purpose for you, get moving to give God the opportunity to direct you along the way!

A large ship is directed by a very small rudder. As you begin to make choices and move forward in your life, listening to the voice of God will gently move the rudder of your ship to steer your course in the right direction toward God's ultimate plan.

Overcomplicating the process will only paralyze us with fear and render us incapable of making decisions!

Remember:
PROMISE = PURPOSE = DESTINY

You are created for a special and unique purpose that is all your own. When Oprah interviewed Barry Manilow several years ago, he revealed to her that all great people *know* deep within themselves that they have been called to a special purpose. This calling is a knowing, something from within, "a knowing without knowing" that you are on the right path to pursue your passion and destiny, even if all of the odds are against you.

If you have that type of deep intuition about your life's purpose, don't let go of it for anything.

Your Purpose Calls to You

(Genesis 12:1) **Now the LORD had said unto Abram...**
In this verse, it says that "God HAD said", which implies that Abraham had heard or felt a guidance within his spirit from God at some time prior. Abraham had clearly been having ongoing conversations with his Creator about his purpose. This small yet

entirely significant example shows that Abraham did not experience some monumental occurrence or "burning bush" experience to direct him to purpose, but rather experienced an inner guidance from the voice of God.

Although many of us never begin the path to our promise because we are waiting on the heavens to open or some other monumental occurrence, the voice of God that Abraham heard was the still, small voice, similar to when God spoke to Elijah in the Scriptures below:

(1 Kings 19:11) **And he [God] said, Go forth, and stand upon the mount before Jehovah. And, behold, Jehovah passed by, and a great and strong wind rent the mountains, and brake in pieces the rocks before Jehovah; but Jehovah was not in the wind: and after the wind an earthquake; but Jehovah was not in the earthquake...**

(1 Kings 19:12) **And after the earthquake a fire; but Jehovah was not in the fire: and after the fire a still small voice.**

(1 Kings 19:13) **And it was so, when Elijah heard it, that he wrapped his face in his mantle, and went out, and stood in the entrance of the cave. And, behold, there came a voice unto him, and said, What doest thou here, Elijah?** (ASV)

Sometimes finding God's purpose for our lives is really that simple. When we get back to the heart of God, which is to enjoy us and have a relationship with us, it becomes easy to tune in to and listen to God's voice as He guides us through life. It is in those simple and quiet times that we can listen to our hearts, ponder our dreams, and hear direct guidance from God to lead us in the next step on our journey.

The fact that God *had spoken* to Abraham could also denote that God, when imparting the vision, also imparted to Abraham the belief in the vision, or the faith necessary to prepare him for his walk with God. Abraham not only received a call from God, he also received a belief (faith) in the promise to carry him to his end destination. The innate belief from within was the catalyst that propelled him on his journey.

(Romans 12:3) **For I say, through the grace given to me, to everyone who is among you, not to think of himself more highly than he ought to think, but to think soberly, as God has dealt to each one a measure of faith.** (NKJV)

This verse clearly states that we have all been given our own measure of faith. When you hear the voice of God guiding you toward His purpose for you, follow him because He has already equipped you with all that you need to get there. Individual guidance from God may appear to each person differently, yet it is the same driving force that will bring us to our destination.

Remember, Abraham is no different from any of us today. You have received the same calling from God. You hear the voice of God guiding you, and you must use your God-given faith to pursue His purpose for your life.

In order to do this, we must develop an "internal ear" that is fine-tuned to hear the subtle voice of God guiding and directing us toward our purpose. As you hear God's voice, you will move forward, based upon what some would call your gut-feeling or intuition, without any physical evidence—that, is the process of faith.

At times, it may be difficult to hear the still, small voice of God, but it is the only true compass to guide you along your journey to your destiny.

God has promised to us what He intends for us to have and nothing less. God will not settle for anything less than His ultimate purpose for our lives, but we might if we are not willing to pursue it. Make no mistake, if we experience anything in our lives that is less than God's abundant promise, it is because we have not yet fully believed and acted on God's purpose for us.

The good news is that God will continue to call until the work is completed. God is there, He is calling—can you hear His call for your life?

Now that you understand how to hear the voice of God to pursue your destiny, it is time to discuss the particulars of God's Promise to you.

For Meditation: How did God equip Abraham for his assignment? How does God equip you? What do you feel is your purpose in life?

(Ephesians 1:11) **In Him also we have obtained an inheritance, being predestined according to the purpose of Him who works all things according to the counsel of His will,** (NKJV)

(Isaiah 43:1) **But now, this is what the LORD says-- he who created you, O Jacob, he who formed you, O Israel: "Fear not, for I have redeemed you; I have summoned you by name; you are mine.** (NIV)

(Isaiah 43:7) **Everyone who is called by My name, Whom I have created for My glory; I have formed him, yes, I have made him."** (NKJV)

3

THE PARTICULARS OF THE PROMISE

(Genesis 17:4-7) **"As for me, this is my covenant with you: You shall be the ancestor of a multitude of nations. No longer shall your name be Abram, but your name shall be Abraham; for I have made you the ancestor of a multitude of nations. I will make you exceedingly fruitful; and I will make nations of you, and kings shall come from you. I will establish my covenant between me and you, and your offspring after you throughout their generations, for an everlasting covenant, to be God to you and to your offspring after you."** (NRSV)

It is said that "the devil is in the details," meaning that most people encounter problems and are deceived because they don't take the time to read the fine print of an agreement. That's why all Bibles should be in LARGE PRINT... -B. R.

T o better understand God's Promise to us through Abraham, we can compare it to a modern-day contract. When entering into any type of agreement, like buying a house, starting a business partnership, or even signing up for a membership or subscription, it is important to understand all terms and conditions of the contract, right?

In the same way, we can learn more about God's Promise to us by understanding the terms and conditions of His contract, or covenant, that He gave to Abraham.

(Genesis 12:1) **Now the LORD had said unto Abram, Get thee out of thy country, and from thy kindred, and from thy father's house, unto a land that I will shew thee...**

(Genesis 12:2) **And I will make of thee a great nation, and I will bless thee, and make thy name great; and thou shalt be a blessing...**

(Genesis 12:3) **And I will bless them that bless thee, and curse him that curseth thee: and in thee shall all families of the earth be blessed.** (KJV)

From the above verses, we can gather that God promised Abraham a new land, a great nation, and a blessed people.

God's Promise can be defined as:

Promise: A pledge to do or not do something specific.

In God's agreement with Abraham, His promise was a contract or covenant that was bound by specific terms and conditions. A contract is defined as an agreement that is made up of a promise, or set of promises, between two parties, in which one will do or refrain from doing a particular thing.

In the Bible, there are two very different types of covenants:

Promissory: God binds Himself to the covenant or oath, which is an unconditional agreement. This promissory covenant depends entirely upon God's Promise.

Obligatory: The people are bound by the covenant or law, which is conditional and depends upon the obedience of the people.

In God's promise to Abraham above, it is promissory and not based upon Abraham's actions. All Abraham had to do was accept the promise to receive all of the blessings God had in store for him. An obligatory promise would be similar to the covenant God created in Malachi 3 for tithing, where God states that He will bless the people if they tithe:

(Malachi 3:10) **Bring the whole tithe into the storehouse, that there may be food in my house. Test me in this," says the LORD Almighty, "and see if I will not throw open the floodgates of heaven and pour out so much blessing that you will not have room enough for it.**

The covenant is based on the supreme power and integrity of God. Within a covenant, when one of the parties is infinitely superior to the other, such as in the covenant between God and man, there God's covenant assumes the nature of the promise.

But what makes this contract or covenant binding between God and us? How do we know that we can trust in this promise given by God thousands of years ago to our spiritual ancestor Abraham? We can gain clarity into covenants, by observing aspects of our legal system.

Here are the necessary components to make a binding contract between two parties:

An offer

An acceptance

Consideration

Within this contractual agreement, the offeree is the person to whom the offer is made. In this instance, it is Abraham. The offeror is the person making the offer, which is God.

The consideration is the reason that a person will choose to enter into a contract in the first place. What will this person be given in exchange for their service or promise of services? What price will they have to pay to receive the promise?

In God's Promise to Abraham, the promise was null and void if Abraham did not live up to his end of the bargain. The Promise was Abraham's regardless, but the only thing that would keep him from receiving it was if Abraham did not receive or go after the promise.

Since this promise from God has been passed on to us, if we do not fulfill our obligations of pursuing God's purpose, then God is not obligated to give His promise to us. When a contract imposes legal obligations on the involved parties, the law gives one of the parties a right to void their legal obligation by canceling the contract.

To give you an example, here is the breakdown of God's promise to Adam in the Garden of Eden:

Offer: God chose to give Adam the Garden to care for, providing for him everything that he needed.

Acceptance: Adam should not eat of the Tree of Good and Evil. This acceptance was the equivalent of signing a contract today.

Consideration: Adam could live a life of abundance and fellowship with God if he cared for the garden and did not eat of the tree. This was Adam's reward or payment for agreeing to the contract.

Contract Void: Adam and Eve ate of the tree anyway and voided their contract, losing their right to live in the Garden of Eden in perfect fellowship with God.

Here is how God's promise to Abraham is broken down in the same terms:

Offer: God will bless Abraham and his seed, and all who bless him.

Acceptance: Abraham must leave his home and family and pursue the promise right away!

Consideration: Abraham would be made into a great nation with a great name, and all of the families of the earth would be blessed through his offspring.

Here is another example of a Biblical covenant in Chronicles:

(2Chronicles 7:14) **If my people, which are called by my name, shall humble themselves, and pray, and seek my face, and turn from their wicked ways; then will I hear from heaven, and will forgive their sin, and will heal their land.** (KJV)

God offers to His people to heal their land, but, in order to accept the contract, God's people must humble themselves, pray and seek God's face, and turn from their wicked ways. Once they have done this, then and only then would God hear their prayers from heaven, forgive their sins, and heal their land. However, this contract would be voided when the people returned back to their sinful ways.

To reinforce the validity of God's promises to you, know that a contract is only as good as the person that is signing it.

With that in mind, is there anyone in this universe better to enter into a contract with? Let's consider the character and integrity of God for a moment:

(Numbers 23:19) **God is not a human being, that he should lie, or a mortal, that he should change his mind. Has he promised, and will he not do it? Has he spoken, and will he not fulfill it?** (NRSV)

(Hebrews 6:13) **When God made his promise to Abraham, since there was no one greater for him to swear by, he swore by himself...** (NIV)

There is no greater entity to enter into a contract or covenant with. God is so awesome and capable that He was able to step out of nothing and create the earth that we now live on. In His power, wisdom, and might, God fulfills all of His Promises that He has spoken to us as a people. As the Scriptures clearly state, there was no greater being for God to swear to Abraham by, so He swore by Himself.

Take a moment to let that sink in and truly understand how powerful and binding God's contract to us is.

If a contract is only as good as the parties that sign it, you can literally thank God that He, our perfect god, overlooked our imperfections when He made this covenant agreement with us. None of us are worthy of the good and great blessings that God has promised us, yet we are given them abundantly and freely anyway.

Throughout the Bible, the Promise was given to imperfect people. There has been no one person in the history of time that has measured up or been worthy to receive God's Promise based upon their own merit, other than Jesus.

Adam and Eve: The first Biblical examples of God's covenant quickly broke the agreement and allowed sin to enter into our perfect world.

Moses: He was chosen as God's spokesperson, yet his ability of speech was questionable and his temper sometimes got the best of him.

David: David was chosen as a young shepherd to reign because he had a heart after God. Although at the height of his kingdom, he committed horrible sins against God.

The examples of imperfect people in the Bible receiving God's promises are many. This alone should be greatly encouraging as you pursue God's Purpose for your life since it reiterates the fact that you do not have to be perfect to receive what God has in store for you.

God has based the terms and conditions of His Promises upon His perfection, His integrity, and His power - not your own. This lifts the burden off of your shoulders to allow you to pursue your dreams and desires and live the fulfilling life that God has planned for you!

Understanding the terms and conditions of God's covenant is the first step to pursuing your purpose ordained by God Himself. The next step on your journey will focus on changing your perspective so that you can clearly see God's promises for your life.

For Meditation: How are God's covenants like a contract? How dependable do you see God?

(1 John 2:25) **And this is the promise that he hath promised us, even eternal life.** (KJV)

(Psalms 119:160) **The sum of thy word is truth; and every one of thy righteous ordinances endures for ever.** (RSV)

(2 Peter 3:9) **The Lord is not slack concerning his promise, as some count slackness; but is longsuffering to you-ward, not wishing that any should perish...** (ASV)

(Isaiah 55:8, 9) **For my thoughts are not your thoughts, neither are your ways my ways, saith the LORD. For as the heavens are higher than the earth, so are my ways higher than your ways, and my thoughts than your thoughts.**

(2 Corinthians 1:20) **For in him every one of God's promises is a "Yes." For this reason it is through him that we say the "Amen," to the glory of God.** (NRSV)

(Isaiah 55: 10, 11) **For as the rain cometh down, and the snow from heaven, and returneth not thither, but watereth the earth, and maketh it bring forth and bud, that it may give seed to the sower, and bread to the eater: So shall my word be that goeth forth out of my mouth: it shall not return unto me void, but it shall accomplish that which I please, and it shall prosper in the thing whereto I sent it.** (KJV)

4

THE PROMISE REQUIRES A FRESH PERSPECTIVE

(Genesis 12:1) **Now the LORD had said unto Abram, "Get thee out of thy country, and from thy kindred, and from thy father's house, unto a land that I will shew thee…"**

"When you change the way you look at things, the things you look at change"- Dr. Wayne Dyer

"Progress is impossible without change, and those who cannot change their minds cannot change anything." – George Bernard Shaw

As God began the pilgrimage of Abraham, the man chosen to father a blessed new nation, His first commandment was for Abraham to leave the people and places of his past. These were the things that had a great influence over Abraham's life and had formed him thus far.

When God said to Abraham, "Get thee out", it was an imperative command, one of force that inferred great urgency. God urged Abraham to run with speed and not look back. God ordered Abraham in this way because, as our creator, He was aware of our human nature. God knew that emotional decisions, like leaving the life that you knew behind, can be difficult for us to make.

Because God created us, He understands our limitations; He understands our emotional bonds to our parents, family, and friends. God knows that leaving your social network and comfort zone is difficult, and unless it is done in a decisive and definite manner, it will never be done. This is why God directed Abraham to go and go quickly, lest he become weak and not go at all.

Leave the Old Behind

In God's clear direction to Abraham, He addresses four very distinct things that Abraham must leave behind:

His place (physical location)
His people
His position
His point of view

The last point may not be so obvious at first, but it becomes clear that Abraham must change his perspective if he wanted to go to the new place to which God was taking him. For God to take us in a new direction in our lives, He has to get us to change our thinking and behaviors.

To change your behavior, you must first change your mindset. To change your mindset, begin by changing your environment.

Abraham accomplished this by obeying the first three requests from God to leave his physical location, his people, and his position, which changed his point of view as a result. All of these factors combined formed Abraham's perspective.

In all endeavors, our success is determined by our access to opportunity, our environment (those we surround ourselves with), and our level of commitment. As God commanded Abraham to leave his country and family, He implied that where Abraham currently lived and the people that he lived with were not conducive to the Promise that he would be given by God Himself.

When God said, "Get thee out of thy country", it was roughly translated as: This is not the proper venue or location; this is not the correct arena for you and your abilities to be displayed.

At first glance, it may not seem that, "Get away from your kindred", or leave your family, would be something that God would say. Isn't family the foundation that God builds upon? Regardless of their faults, family is the one thing we all have. After all, Abraham had no say in selecting his own family. Family is the one thing in life that you don't get to choose.

Since God created family, He not only understood this, but He actually designed the deep bonds and influence that family has on how we perceive and respond to situations. God was well aware of the influence of family, so He had to remove Abraham's family influence for him to move forward successfully.

The Promise was not for Abraham's family, but for Abraham. For this reason, Abraham's family could never fully comprehend what Abraham was being called to do, and they may have even become a stumbling block to Abraham.

The Influence of Our Environment

The communities in which we reside, work, worship, or play can either support or oppress us.

These environments will either infuse us with positive energy that spawns creativity and success, or they will empty and deplete us of the lifeblood that God has given to us to inspire others. As a result, these negative environments will deplete all who come into contact with us.

For better or worse, we are products of our environment. God in His wisdom will always seek to protect us from the negative and guide us to better places.

As God began to guide His chosen people to their promised land, he often instructed the Israelites when conquering a new territory to kill all the inhabitants of that land and leave none alive. This may seem cruel and barbaric, but God understood that the inhabitants of a land would influence His chosen people to accept and eventually serve gods other than Himself.

God had the same purpose when he urged Abraham to leave his family and comfortable environment behind to pursue the Promise. Abraham's place or physical location had two components:

1. The influence it exerted upon the residents.

God did not want Abraham to be corrupted by those around him. The country in which Abraham lived had definite patterns of worship, customs, and beliefs that were entrenched in the values of that society. Those values had the power to forever influence and plague Abraham, stifling his fullest potential.

In some cases, family can be a stumbling block to our own lives. We grew up listening and valuing our family's views, and family traditions are often what our lives are built upon, for better or worse. Yet God calls us to follow Him faithfully and without any hindrances from the people in our lives.

(Matthew 10:37) **He that loveth father or mother more than me is not worthy of me: and he that loveth son or daughter more than me is not worthy of me.**

(Matthew 10:38) **And he that taketh not his cross, and followeth after me, is not worthy of me.** (KJV)

The company that we keep can be our greatest influencers, causing us to change the way that we think, feel, and behave. As we begin to pursue God's Promise for our lives, family can actually be one of the greatest detractors. Think about it. Our family has known us all our lives, and many times, they focus upon our problems and not our potential. Our family may not have the capacity to focus on our future because they remain focused on the mistakes of our past.

(Luke 14:26) **If any man come to me, and hate not his father, and mother, and wife, and children, and brethren, and sisters, yea, and his own life also, he cannot be my disciple.** (KJV)

This is God's way of telling us that we must be willing to focus on Him and Him alone, regardless of the influence of our family or any other people in our environment.

2.   The   possibilities   of   opportunities   afforded   the residents.

Success   can   be   defined   as   when   preparation   meets opportunity, or:

Success = Preparation + Opportunity

It really is that simple. As God moves us toward our promise, there must be an opportunity for us to display the abilities that God has blessed us with. Yet for these abilities to be noticed, they must first be needed. For our abilities to be appreciated, there must first be a need for them.

God longs for us to fulfill our purpose, so He will always place us in a situation that has a need to draw out our God-given abilities. For anyone that has ever found themselves in a dead-end job or limited by a glass ceiling, then you know firsthand that you could have more skill and ability than anyone in your workplace, but, if you are not given the opportunity to display your talents, it is the same as not having the talent at all.

As   we   proceed   to   the   promise,   God   assumes   the responsibility of creating a venue, a place that has a problem and a need that can only be solved by YOU.

God directs us to this designated place with a designated need that will allow our God-given talents and abilities to not only be discovered but to be appreciated.

The Power of Your Perspective

God ordered Abraham to leave his country, father's house, and position. These combined changes would bring about a new perspective or outlook.

Abraham would no longer be able to stand in his position as son, but now he would be thrust to the forefront as the father of a great nation. In his past travels, Abraham had already experienced that his position as son was inadequate. He had operated in a subservient position, but now he was called to lead. Instead of following in his father's footsteps, Abraham would now lead as a father. Instead of taking directions from his earthly father, Abraham would now listen intently for directions from his Heavenly Father.

Now that Abraham's position had changed, his responsibilities had changed as a result. Instead of looking at everything in the present, Abraham must now view the future and how the decisions of his new position would affect his future.

Just as an employee promoted to management will always remember the lessons he learned as a follower, he will find that he must now think differently as a member of the management team. Although he is the same person, he now operates at a different rung of the corporate ladder. His position and view has now changed, causing his perspective to change with it.

Psychiatrists understand the need for change in environment and mindset. They will often recommend that their clients make minor changes in their daily rituals to facilitate a greater change in their daily lives.

It is impossible to change one's life while repeating the same actions again and again.

Just like the old adage says, "When you keep on doing what you've been doing, you keep on getting what you've been getting." You may also be familiar with the saying that the definition of insanity is repeating the same actions again and again while getting the same result.

To create a great change in our lives, we need a new perspective and a new mindset. We must first believe to achieve. If we are limited by our old thoughts, we will never reach the new levels for which we have been designed.

When Jesus was speaking to his disciples in Luke 5:37-39, he told his listeners that new revelations could not be stored in old containers.

(Luke 5:37) **And no man putteth new wine into old bottles; else the new wine will burst the bottles, and be spilled, and the bottles shall perish.**

(38) **But new wine must be put into new bottles; and both are preserved.** (KJV)

If we are to act differently, we must first think differently. To think differently, our heart and mind must be changed. We cannot do new things using old ways and old thoughts. Just as we have become new creatures after giving our life over to Christ, Abraham also became a new creature as he gave his life over to God's purpose for him.

As you feel God's call on your life urging you to step away from your comfortable environment, take courage in the fact that God is drawing you toward a need that will tap into your greater purpose. When you feel God's urge guiding you in a new direction, it is time to cast aside the old and embrace the new to experience true transformation on your journey to the Promise.

For Meditation: What comfort zone might you need to leave behind to pursue God's promise? What did Abraham leave behind? How can you learn from him? What did Jesus say about this?

(Philippians 3:13-14) **Brethren, I do not regard myself as having laid hold of it yet; but one thing I do: forgetting what lies behind and reaching forward to what lies ahead, I press on toward the goal for the prize of the upward call of God in Christ Jesus.** (NAS95)

(Philippians 4:8) **Finally, brethren, whatsoever things are true, whatsoever things are honest, whatsoever things are just, whatsoever things are pure, whatsoever things are lovely, whatsoever things are of good report; if there be any virtue, and if there be any praise, think on these things.** (KJV)

5

THE PROMISE HAS ONLY ONE PREREQUISITE

(Hebrews 11:8) **By faith Abraham, when he was called, obeyed by going out to a place which he was to receive for an inheritance; and he went out, not knowing where he was going.** (NASB)

Never worry about whether those around you believe and trust in you. YOUR success has nothing to do with what they believe- but everything to do with what you believe!!! DO YOU BELIEVE?? - BR

A fter taking a deeper look at the story of Abraham, it poses an interesting question. If humans had been in charge of the hiring, would Abraham have made it through the hiring process? It seems doubtful.

Imagine Abraham showing up at a recruitment agency to apply for the position of "Father of God's Chosen Nation". He had no previous job experience, no prestigious pedigree, and no prior training on his resume. Even though his family lineage wasn't given in the Bible, Abraham did not appear to come from a royal or connected family or even a long line of high achievers.

Abraham was the average Joe Blow that put his pants on one leg at a time, just like everyone else. He enjoyed the same things that other men enjoyed, and he likely even spilled food on his tie from time to time. So what made Abraham so special in the eyes of God?

For a job as important as the father of God's chosen people, it would seem that God would have selected a special person, one who'd been specially prepared and bred for this assignment; someone who had the necessary training and previous experience to qualify. Perhaps God would have chosen someone with an advanced degree in "fathering a nation" to prove his skills and qualifications.

Yet out of all of the people that God could have chosen, He chose Abraham. God chose Abraham because Abraham did posses something, some intrinsic value, something that was not seen by human eyes yet was recognized solely by the Creator of all.

How can we forget the story of Samuel's search for the new king to replace Saul? In 1 Samuel 16:7, it says that Samuel the prophet was instructed by the Lord to visit the house of Jesse and choose from among his sons. However, in choosing Samuel was instructed not to look on his countenance or on the height of his stature.

(1Samuel 16:7) **But the LORD said to Samuel, "Do not look on his appearance or on the height of his stature... for the LORD sees not as man sees; man looks on the outward appearance, but the LORD looks on the heart."** (RSV)

This scripture sheds great light on God and his selection process. God is never moved by outward appearance, but rather by inner virtues, namely a humble, submissive and willing heart.

Faith Sets You Apart

Throughout the Bible, faith was the quality that made Abraham special in the eyes of God. Faith is defined as a belief in the value and trustworthiness of someone or something: confidence, trust, and assurance.

We can see evidence of Abraham's faith in Scripture:

(Romans 4:3) **For what does the scripture say? "Abraham believed God, and it was reckoned to him as righteousness."**

(Romans 4:13) **The promise to Abraham and his descendants, that they should inherit the world, did not come through the law but through the righteousness of faith.** (RSV)

It is important to point out that it was not the object of his faith that made Abraham special, but it was the *action* of his faith that secured his position as the father of the promise. Romans 4:13 tells us that the promise to Abraham and his descendants came through Abraham's righteousness of faith. Romans 4:3 further clarifies that Abraham was considered righteous simply because he believed in God.

Abraham's faith, which was defined as the belief in the trustworthiness of something or someone (God), caused Abraham to believe. Because Abraham believed, he obeyed God, plain and simple. To make it even clearer, God chose Abraham because He knew Abraham would go.

God's promises are only limited by your actions, and are only nullified by your inactions.

There are so many things left undone in the world today because so many of us allow ourselves to be defined by the views of others. We often see ourselves as others see us, through the harsh eyes of human criticism rather than the heart of divine grace. We view ourselves in terms of what we feel we are lacking: we're not pretty enough, not tall enough, not smart enough—and the list goes on and on. But by human standards, we will never be enough.

When we think this way about ourselves, we are actually questioning what God, in His all-knowing, all-present, and all-powerful state, has chosen to create and ordain for His purpose and time. When we think this way, we are essentially saying, "God, you have placed me here ill-equipped and unprepared. God, are you sure?"

The main reason people fail to move into their promise is a lack of faith in themselves, which is actually a lack of faith in God.

When God spoke to Jeremiah in chapter 1, Verse 5, God showed Jeremiah that before he was even formed and before he was even conceived, God knew Jeremiah's purpose and had prepared him for that time. From the very beginning, Jeremiah possessed everything that he needed to succeed at his assigned task. This reinforces the fact that where God guides, He provides.

In the book of John, after Jesus had spent an entire day ministering to the multitudes, his disciples came to him and suggested that he send the crowd home because the hour was growing late and no one had eaten that day. Jesus, true to form, decided to give the disciples a "pop quiz", suggesting that rather than sending the multitudes away, the disciples should prepare dinner for them.

The disciples, like so many of us, viewed things from a human perspective of doubt rather than a divine perspective of faith. They focused on the problems rather than the possibilities.

Jesus then suggested that rather than giving up, the disciples take a moment to evaluate the resources that they already possessed to perform the necessary task at hand. After a scavenger hunt through the crowd of 5,000 men plus women and children, Simon Peter's brother, Andrew, returned with a young lad and his small sack lunch.

The disciples were still plagued by doubts and negativity, questioning, "What good is so little in the face of such great need?" The disciples, who had seen firsthand how Jesus specialized in doing so much with little, should have known better. After Jesus blessed the food, he gave it to his disciples and instructed them to serve it to the multitudes. After everyone had eaten their fill, there were 12 baskets of scraps left over.

We Must Claim the Promise

This story highlights a wonderful Biblical principle that is key to understanding our promise and purpose here on this Earth. Because God created us for each and every situation that we will face, He is never concerned about what we lack. On the contrary, God wants us to use what we have.

Our promise will never be realized, and our purpose will never be fulfilled to bless others, until we present back to God what He has given to us.

Just as Moses went before Pharaoh with nothing more than a stick in his hand and a stuttering in his tongue…

Just as David faced down the giant Goliath with a sling and five smooth stones…

Just as Queen Esther went before the King with a mere belief that she had been created "for such a time as this"…

We have all been created and called forth with nothing more than "what we have" been equipped to give.

Our individual promise was given to us by God, and there is nothing that we have to do to receive it. There is also nothing we can do to change or void this promise granted to us by the Creator. However, for us to receive our promise, we must claim it by possessing the necessary faith to believe and move forward.

We have this amazing promise from God right in front of us today. As was evident in the story of Jesus feeding the 5,000, it is easy for us to follow in the steps of the disciples and let human doubt get the best of us. The good news is that God's promise is real. God's promise is available, and God's promise has been granted to us not based on our own merit or aptitude.

The only prerequisite to God's promise is that we must have faith and move forward to receive it.

For Meditation: How would you define faith? Why is faith important?

(Mark 9:23) **Jesus said to him, If you can believe, all things are possible to him who believes.** (MKJV)

(Mark 11:22-23) **Jesus answered them, "Have faith in God. Truly I tell you, if you say to this mountain, 'Be taken up and thrown into the sea,' and if you do not doubt in your heart,** but believe that what you say will come to pass, it will be done for you. (NRSV)

(Matthew 7:7-8) **Ask, and it shall be given you; seek, and ye shall find; knock, and it shall be opened unto you: For everyone that asketh receiveth; and he that seeketh findeth; and to him that knocketh it shall be opened.** (KJV)

(James 1:6) **...But let him ask in faith, with no doubting, for he who doubts is like a wave of the sea that is driven and tossed by the wind.** (RSV)

6

THE PROMISE GIVER EXPECTS A PROFIT

(Genesis 24:35) **And the LORD has blessed my master [Abraham] greatly, and he has become great. And He has given him flocks and herds and silver and gold, and male slaves and slave women, and camels and asses.** (MKJV)

If you count all your assets, you always show a profit.
-Robert Quillen
Every business seeks to maximize its' profits...Each person should seek to maximize their potential. -B. R.

T o describe God as a businessman may be met with cries of blasphemy. But that is just what He is.

The very first point that they teach in business school is the concept of profit. The number one rule and the ultimate goal of any business organization is to make a profit for its shareholders.

Profit can be defined as:

Realizing an advantage or reward; to possess more of something at the end than you had at the beginning, or to simply gain something in the process.

Would you be surprised to know that the kingdom of heaven is based upon a profit system? God makes a great—but relatively small in the grand scheme of things—investment in each one of us, the people of His promise. His desire and intent is to generate a major profit for His kingdom.

God as a businessman—is it really that preposterous?

When Jesus spoke of his father's kingdom, he spoke of profit without shame. He stated plainly that each of us, before the closing of time, would be judged on our profits brought to the King, as stated in Matthew:

(Matthew 25:14) **For the kingdom of heaven is as a man travelling into a far country, who called his own servants, and delivered unto them his goods.**

(Mt 25:15) **To one he gave five talents, to another two, to another one, to each according to his ability. Then he went away.**

(Mt 25:16) **The one who had received the five talents went off at once and traded with them, and made five more talents.**

(Mt 25:17) **In the same way, the one who had the two talents made two more talents.**

(Mt 25:18) **But the one who had received the one talent went off and dug a hole in the ground and hid his master's money.**

(Mt 25:19) **After a long time the master of those slaves came and settled accounts with them.**

(Mt 25:20) **Then the one who had received the five talents came forward, bringing five more talents, saying, 'Master, you handed over to me five talents; see, I have made five more talents.'**

(Mt 25:21) **His master said to him, 'Well done, good and trustworthy slave; you have been trustworthy in a few things, I will put you in charge of many things; enter into the joy of your master.'**

(Mt 25:22) **And the one with the two talents also came forward, saying, 'Master, you handed over to me two talents; see, I have made two more talents.'**

(Mt 25:23) **His master said to him, 'Well done, good and trustworthy slave; you have been trustworthy in a few things, I will put you in charge of many things; enter into the joy of your master.'**

(Mt 25:24) **Then the one who had received the one talent also came forward, saying, 'Master, I knew that you were a harsh man, reaping where you did not sow, and gathering where you did not scatter seed;**

(Mt 25:25) **so I was afraid, and I went and hid your talent in the ground. Here you have what is yours.'**

(Mt 25:26) **But his master replied, 'You wicked and lazy slave! You knew, did you, that I reap where I did not sow, and gather where I did not scatter?**

(Mt 25:27) **Then you ought to have invested my money with the bankers, and on my return I would have received what was my own with interest.**

(Mt 25:28) **So take the talent from him, and give it to the one with the ten talents.**

(Mt 25:29) **For to all those who have, more will be given, and they will have an abundance; but from those who have nothing, even what they have will be taken away.**

(Mt 25:30) **As for this worthless slave, throw him into the outer darkness, where there will be weeping and gnashing of teeth.'** (NRSV)

This Scripture brings us to the following conclusions:

1. Jesus draws a parallel, comparing the parable to the kingdom of God. In other words, the principle of the parable corresponds to the principle of entering the kingdom of God.

2. In Verse 15, the Lord gave to each man according to his own ability. Notice that each participant received a certain amount but not the same amount. Each servant was given according to his or her own ability and purpose.

3. Each person was then given time and opportunity to invest and increase; they were expected to profit from what had been entrusted to each of them.

4. Upon returning, the Lord then called all who had been given an opportunity to be evaluated.

5. Those that had taken the initial investment and made a profit were told that what they had done was good. They were told "well done" and described as good and faithful servants.

6. However, the one servant that made no profit and returned the Lord's original investment was called wicked and slothful. Because he was an unprofitable servant, he was cast out of the kingdom to regret his mistake forever.

How God Views Profit

We can get a greater understanding of how God views profit in the Old Testament:

(Isaiah 48:17) **Thus says the LORD, your Redeemer, the Holy One of Israel: "I am the LORD your God, who teaches you to profit, who leads you in the way you should go.**

(Ecclesiastes 5:9) **Moreover the profit of the earth is for all: the king himself is served by the field.**

Make no mistake that our promise and purpose have been given to us by God to be a blessing to the world. What God gives to us is the equivalent of an initial investment - a smaller amount that is intended to increase in value at the completion of its term.

It is a sin to remain stagnant or static; God expects us to take the abilities He has given to us as an investment, use them, and ultimately bless those that we come into contact with. This chain of events pleases God greatly.

Yes, God invests in each of us by forming and creating us for a specific task. He equips us with the necessary abilities and then releases us into the world or marketplace to perform His will here on this earth.

This theory of profit is seen throughout the Scripture and evidenced in the above examples. Time and time again, when people came into contact with God and his Son, they were blessed and left with more than they started with. It is true, when we serve God we always get more than we could possibly give.

In Matthew 6:33, Jesus tells us that if we "first seek the kingdom of God and his righteousness; then ALL these things will be added to our lives". If we do the one task of seeking first God's kingdom, THEN all these things will be added to us. The concept of profit is embedded in this scripture as well; by doing one thing, seeking God first, we in turn receive all things.

In Malachi 3, we are told that if we give back a portion of our worldly possessions, which are the goods that God has already blessed us with, God will give back to us much more than we could ever give to Him. This brings us back to the Biblical principle that we will always reap more than we sow. This clearly indicates that God's purpose for profit is not what we can do for Him but what HE can do for us to enrich our lives and allow us to bless others.

Abraham is the first example of the initial investment that God made in His people. By Abraham giving himself over to God, Abraham not only profited by receiving riches, a great name, and a family that was as abundant as the sands of the seashore, BUT God also received profit in His chosen people.

To discuss profit or wealth is seen as inappropriate by many people, especially within Christian circles because it appears that we are placing more emphasis on wealth than on God. However, that attitude has resulted in generations of believers that live life like the servant that was given the one talent; they have no aspirations of bettering their life and the lives of others. Yet the truth is, based on all of the Scripture that we have seen throughout this book, God wants to give us more than we have ever asked for - but we aren't asking for it!

The previous chapter taught us that we must have the faith to reach out and claim God's promise for our lives. The next step is to expect the blessings of God as we do so. God wants to profit and bless us greatly because we are His chosen people. As God showers His abundance on our lives, we will have the capacity to fulfill our purpose and enrich the lives of the people around us.

Don't make the mistake of neglecting God's investment within you.

God has placed something truly special within you, but you must pursue this purpose to receive God's abundant promise!

For Meditation: What has God invested in you? What does he expect back as profit? How can you profit from God's guidance?

(John 15:16) **You did not choose me but I chose you. And I appointed you to go and bear fruit...** (NRSV)

(Deuteronomy 7:9) **Know therefore that the LORD your God is God, the faithful God who maintains covenant loyalty with those who love him and keep his commandments, to a thousand generations,** (NRSV)

(1 Corinthians 12:6-7) **And there are diversities of operations, but it is the same God which worketh all in all. But the manifestation of the Spirit is given to every man to profit withal.** (KJV)

7

PROMISED PEOPLE OFTEN APPEAR PECULIAR

(Deuteronomy 14:2) **For thou [art] an holy people unto the LORD thy God, and the LORD hath chosen thee to be a peculiar people unto himself, above all the nations that [are] upon the earth.**

Always remember that you are absolutely unique. Just like everyone else. -Margaret Mead

P eculiar, odd, or strange may not be terms that we would often consider flattering to the people of God. However, these are the terms that best describe the people of God.

While it is the desire of many people who follow God to be considered normal, when you look back in the Bible, you will find that all of God's people were far from normal. As a matter of fact, when looking back through the Bible, you will find that the people who agreed to accept God's call also lived the most peculiar lives.

FACT: To live a life of uncommon promise, you will be called to do uncommon things.

There are many people who spend their lives trying to be like everyone else. Everyone wants to be considered normal, when all that does is diminish our God-given uniqueness. Remember, we were given a specific promise and chosen for a specific purpose, so it would stand to reason that each of us was created differently from all other beings that walk this earth.

Since we have all received specific promises based upon what we are to accomplish in our lifetimes, our lives will never be identical to anyone else's. If we are to be successful in what we are called to do, it requires marching to the beat of our own drum since our inner song is different from all the other songs that are playing.

Uniqueness is not just God's special gift to us, but it is a *requirement* to fulfill God's unique promise.

A Rare and Uncommon People

To give you an example, think of the car that you drive. As you drive down the road and look around you, which car has the most worth? Is it a Chevy or a Lamborghini? How many people out there actually drive these exotic sports cars? The next time that you're out on the road, count the number of Chevys, Fords and other commonly seen cars that are being used by the majority of people heading to work and going about their daily tasks.

There is absolutely nothing wrong with driving a Ford, Chevy, or Dodge, but driving an exotic sports car like a Lamborghini is extremely rare. What gives a Lamborghini its worth is the fact that there are so few of them made; these cars are exquisite, rare jewels amongst a field of rocks.

So why do each of us want to be like Fords or Chevys and remain commonplace in today's society? This is the choice that we make when we aspire to be just like everyone else, "normal" or "status quo". It is time for people to stand up and be who they were called to be by God—a rare and uncommon human being.

A friend once shared with me the details of his call to ministry. He told me the story of how when God called him to ministry, he attempted to bargain with God. He would only accept God's call to preach (the uncommon and uncompromising) Word of God as long as God did not call him to be different, uncommon or out of sync with the people around him.

Although I understood what my friend meant, that he didn't want to live a strange life walking around the wilderness wearing camel's hair and eating wild locust and honey like John the Baptist, he still simply aspired to be just like the next guy.

My question to my friend and to you is that if the gospel is uncommon, and the tasks for which you've been created are uncommon, wouldn't you as a result have to be uncommon to live your life of purpose? As we look back through the examples in the Bible, we find that all of God's special servants were undeniably uncommon. And that was a good thing.

(Deuteronomy 26:18) **And the LORD has taken you today to be His peculiar people, as He has promised you...** (MKJV)

Imagine how peculiar those who were chosen for a great task in the service of God must have seemed to those around them. Imagine Moses trying to convince the Hebrew slaves to follow him out of Egypt. It may have gone something like this:

Slaves: "Now, Moses, tell us again who sent you?"
Moses: "I AM."
Slaves: "Yes, but He is... who?"
Moses: "I AM."
Slaves: "We know, but He is who?"
Moses: "I AM..."

Slaves: "Moses, you're making this too hard… Now what did He say His name was?"

Moses: "I just told you, I AM."

Slaves: "Moses, He said, 'I am 'what'?'"

Moses: "That's what I said at first. When I asked Him who I should say sent me, He said, 'Tell them, 'I am that I AM.'"

Slaves: *in disgust* "I am WHO?"

Moses may have said something like this:

"The wildest thing happened to me today. I was out tending cattle on the backside of the desert when I came upon a burning bush, and I swear it was burning yet it was never consumed."

"What do you mean not consumed?"

"I mean… It just burned… and burned… and burned… But it never burned away."

"Moses, what time of day was this? I mean… were you off work? Was it already cocktail hour?"

Or would you rather have been David going out to fight Goliath?

"I will not let that dirty Philistine talk about my God."

"Well, what are you going to do?"

"I'm going to defend the honor of my God!"

"You mean, YOU are?"

"That's what I said."

"Not your big brother, but you…?"

"Yes, me!"

Everyone laughs *"And how tall are you? Anyway, how much do you weigh? Maybe you should rethink this. If we're still here in a few years, maybe you can fight that giant Goliath then."*

Or how would you like to have been Abraham trying to explain to his wife and family that he had been called to go to a country that he'd never seen?

"I called this family meeting to let you all know that God has told me to go to another country. We're going to be packing up the family and leaving, and I just wanted to let you know."

"Okay, so where are you going?"

"Well… I really don't know."

"Come on, Abraham, you can tell us where you're going. If you don't want to be specific, just tell us if it's in Ur or in Canaan. Just give us a general idea of where it is."

"I'm not really sure."

"So how will you know where to go?"

"God will direct me."

"Which god? Baal? Or one of the other gods?"

"No, it's not one of those gods."

"Well, which God is it?" (as all of Abraham's family members look at each other quizzically.)

"I'm not sure; He just kind of speaks to me in my head...more like my heart... I just kind of know what He's saying."

"So let me get this straight. You're going to a place you've never seen, that you're not sure even exists, because you believe you were directed to go there by a God that nobody around here has ever heard of?"

"Yeah, I know it sounds crazy, but that's about it..."

The path to purpose and promise is new and uncharted territory, a solemn and lonely road that was created for you and you alone. Although you may begin this journey encouraged by a crowd of loved ones and well-wishers, the bulk of your travel will be done alone, amidst accusations of foul and folly.

Stay on Course

Thank God that many chose to stay on their path no matter what others thought, no matter how peculiar they might have seemed. While Orville had his brother Wilbur Wright to help him build their flying contraption that would prepare the way for the multibillion dollar airplane industry of today, he likely desired someone other than his brother to believe that man could fly.

Henry Ford was called many things on the way to inventing the horseless carriage; peculiar was likely one of the most generous.

Martin Luther King was termed a misfit and troublemaker because he encouraged others to join him in marching to the beat of a different drum.

Gandhi not only defied the British government, eventually ending centuries of oppression and poverty, but he radically defied conventional wisdom of how war must be fought.

No, it wasn't that these visionaries and shapers of history were peculiar; they were actually common everyday people. Common people within an uncommon promise that rose above destructive comments and condemning sneers of family, friends, and onlookers to fulfill their God-given purpose. In that way, they were peculiar. Dare to be peculiar, you'll find yourself in very good company!

For Meditation: How might you find yourself bargaining with God? If you wish to pursue God's promise for you, what must you be prepared for as regards your family and friends? How can you prepare yourself for such a situation?

(John 15:19) **If ye were of the world, the world would love his own: but because ye are not of the world, but I have chosen you out of the world, therefore the world hateth you.** (KJV)

(1 Peter 2:9) **But you are a chosen race, a royal priesthood, a holy nation, God's own people, in order that you may proclaim the mighty acts of him who called you out of darkness into his marvelous light.** (NRSV)

8

THE PROMISE IS PERSONAL BUT NOT PRIVATE

(Ge 12:2) **And I will make of thee a great nation, and I will bless thee...**

(Ge 12:3) **... and in thee shall all families of the earth be blessed.** (KJV)

When God blesses us with talents and abilities, they are like a field of beautiful flowers or a great scenic view. No matter how majestic or how beautiful; until someone comes in contact with it, and experiences the beauty, it is just another field of flowers or scenic view. So are the promises of God; of no effect until they are encountered by those we are sent to bless. -BR

O ne of the basic principles we must always keep in mind is that the promise, although given to us, is never really about us.

In Genesis chapter 3 verse 2, when placing the great blessing over Abraham's life, God tells Abraham, "I will bless thee... and thou shalt be a blessing." In Verse 3, God says, "I will bless them that bless thee and curse them that curse thee: and in thee all the families of the earth shall be blessed."

It doesn't take much study to understand that although Abraham received the actual blessing, the blessing was not intended to benefit him alone but rather *all* people of the earth.

By using the balance sheet approach, we find that the world benefited much more from the promise than Abraham did himself. Consider this:

Benefits to Abraham—I will bless thee... Make thy name great...

Benefits to the World—I will make of thee a great nation...And thou shalt be a blessing.. All families of the earth be blessed...I will bless them that bless thee... and curse him that curseth thee...

It appears that more of the promise was related to others than to Abraham.

It seemed that Abraham was really a means or method of the process and not the end recipient: Abraham was utilized to fulfill the promise of God.

From this we make a great revelation, God's plans for your life are not designed for you alone, but to touch the lives of others that you come into contact with here on Earth. Because God is spirit, He utilizes human flesh to complete His work here on Earth, flesh that He ordained before the beginning of time to fulfill the specific tasks for which we were created.

The Right Place at the Right Time

In the Book of Acts, chapter 8, it tells the story of Philip, who desired to go to Asia Minor to preach to the populations there. However, God spoke to him in a dream at night and sent Philip in the complete opposite direction, down the lonely desert stretch of road that led from Jerusalem to Gaza.

On the road, Philip encountered an Ethiopian eunuch, who was struggling to make sense of his reading in the book of Isaiah. Then God spoke to Philip and told him to go run alongside the chariot. Interestingly enough, as it often happens with the things of God, Philip arrived in the right place, at the right time, with exactly what was needed to touch someone's life.

Philip then asked, "Do you understand what you are reading?" The Ethiopian eunuch replied, "How can I understand unless some man helps me?"

Philip desired to go to Asia, but God needed him to walk along a desert highway to meet a dignitary of the great Queen of Ethiopia. By following the lead of God, Philip became the catalyst to send the gospel into new lands that had never heard the good news.

It is only when we realize that our promise, which is based upon a specific purpose, is God's means of carrying out His will here on earth that we can understand our true purpose. In the end, the promise is not given to only bring blessings to us but to bring blessings through us. Our promise will become purpose when, and only when, we realize that what we have been given, although personal, was never meant to be private.

This truth can only be realized when we reach out to help those who are in need.

Just like the Ethiopian eunuch, there are countless people trapped, oppressed, or aimlessly wandering through this life, waiting for some man or woman to run alongside of them and lend a hand.

We Channel God's Blessings

It is important that we notice how the direction of God's blessings flows:

God blesses Abraham (God to Abraham)

God blesses others through Abraham (God to Abraham to Others)

Others will be blessed or cursed by how they treat Abraham (God to Abraham to Others to Abraham)

Not only was Abraham the recipient of the blessing, but he was also the conduit by which the blessings would flow. Just as Abraham was used as a conduit through which the blessings of God would flow, so are we to be used today.

Remember, what you have been given, is your way of blessings others, so that you in turn may be blessed!

So many of us do not recognize that we are the channel that God uses to bless others in our lives. If you are hoping to receive the blessings of God in your life as you pursue His purpose for you, the only way to do so is by first focusing on blessing those around you.

As you open your channel for God's blessings to flow through you, you will be blessed as a natural byproduct. Instead of seeking God's blessing for your own life without consideration for those around you, you can receive abundant blessings upon blessings simply by giving to those in your life.

God's blessings have a natural chain of events. While God has given you a specific promise for your life that is unique and all yours, this promise and its subsequent blessings will never be kept private. God's promise and His accompanying blessings move through you to impact those around you.

Keep your eyes, ears, and heart open for the many ways that God hopes to bless those around you through you, and in doing so, you too will be blessed.

For Meditation: Think of some ways others can be blessed through you? What does that tell you about the basic way we are all connected? How would it affect you to surround yourself with others that seek God's blessings?

(Proverbs 28:27) **Whoever gives to the poor will lack nothing, but one who turns a blind eye will get many a curse.** (NRSV)

(Proverbs 13:20) **He that walketh with wise men shall be wise: but a companion of fools shall be destroyed.**

9

PROCRASTINATION ONLY DELAYS THE PROMISE

(Genesis 12:4) **So Abram departed, as the LORD had spoken unto him...**

(Genesis 17:23) **Then Abraham took Ishmael his son and all the slaves born in his house or bought with his money, every male among the men of Abraham's house, and he circumcised the flesh of their foreskins that very day, as God had said to him.** (RSV)

Procrastination is opportunity's assassin. -Victor Kiam

Tomorrow is often the busiest day of the week.-Spanish Proverb

P rocrastination is a choice that will cause your promise to be delayed. While putting off what God is calling you to do today may offer a false temporary pleasure, it is a choice that could result in prolonged, if not lifetime consequences. Namely, a life that is inferior to what you and God desire.

In Genesis 17: 23, Abraham, who was 99 years old at the time, was instructed to circumcise himself, his son Ishmael, and all the males of his household. This rite, where the foreskin was cut away in each male, would serve as a sign of obedience and establish God's blood covenant with Abraham.

Notice that the Scripture says Abraham obeyed "that very day". The King James Version also says "the same day". No matter what terminology that you use, it means the same thing. Abraham did what he was told, when he was told, without delay.

Abraham was probably keenly aware of the pain that he and every man in his household would have to suffer due to his obedience. As well, Abraham could have rationalized within himself that he had done well without being circumcised for 99 years; why do it now? Nonetheless, Abraham proceeded without procrastination because he realized that any delay in his performance of God's instructions would result in a delay of his promise.

This symbolic ritual allowed Abraham to start his journey fresh by cutting away the old to pursue his promise uninhibited. In the same way, God calls us to be quick in cutting away anything old and dead in our lives that could delay us in the pursuit of the promise.

As God calls you, be ready to act quickly and ask yourself what you may need to cut away to begin your journey fresh and without hindrance. There are some things in life, although painful or frightening, that must be done for the process to proceed; a delay in action will always result in a delay in the process of the promise.

Throughout Abraham's story, we find that he embarked upon every task, followed every instruction, and implemented every plan swiftly and without delay.

In Genesis 12:4, after receiving the promise, Abraham departs for an unknown land.

In Genesis 14:14, the Scripture implies that as soon as Abraham heard of Lott's capture by a foreign army, he assembled his fighting men and rushed to rescue his nephew.

In Genesis 22:3, after being instructed to offer his only son Isaac as a sacrifice on the altar, the Scripture says that Abraham rose early the next morning to fulfill his command.

No matter what the demand, Abraham moved quickly to carry it out.

Why would Abraham, and others like him, march hurriedly into danger? Because they understood that the promise could not be realized until their purpose had been fulfilled. The people of the promise chose to live by faith, having ultimate faith in God. They followed God's own example (when on earth in the form of God the Son) when Jesus refused to run from the promise of a new beginning, no matter how painful. Jesus told Judas in John 13:2 (RSV), "What you are going to do, do quickly."

When approaching Goliath on the battlefield, the Bible says that David ran to meet the giant that threatened to take his life. The willingness and inspiration to carry out God's instruction without procrastination seemed to be a trait that was possessed by all the promised people of God.

The Process Is the First Step

Until we are willing to begin the process when we are called, the journey to the promise can never end. As we discussed in the previous chapter, we are each a channel for God's blessings into the lives of others. There are people who can never be blessed until we begin the process.

More than 30 years ago, in 1978, 5% of the population surveyed admitted that they were chronic procrastinators. In a 2007 survey, 26% of the population confessed to struggling with chronic procrastination; procrastination is on the rise in today's world! Another survey of student populations indicated that procrastination plagues 85-95% of students in their daily lives.

While we may joke about procrastinating or putting off an important task, these same bad habits cannot carry over into our pursuit of the promise. While causes of procrastination can differ, there may be several common triggers of procrastination in our lives:

Fear of failure
Fear of success
Rebellion against authority
Fear of being alone

The common denominator in all of these procrastination triggers is fear. As the Scripture tells us:

(2 Timothy 1:7) **For God gave us a spirit not of fear but of power and love and self-control.**

As we discussed in a previous chapter, God has given you the ability to succeed where you are called. While it is completely natural to have a fear of the unknown, even the unrecognized fear of success, and especially a fear of failure, take courage that Abraham, Moses, and David definitely felt the same emotions when they were called to act on God's plan right away.

Change is never comfortable for anyone, yet it is our willingness to follow God's calling that will bring us to our destination. The first step is to begin the process, no matter what fears may be plaguing us and causing us to procrastinate. By beginning, it shows that we have the faith that we need to complete our journey to God's purpose for our lives.

Lao Tsu, an older contemporary of Confucius, wrote in the Tao Te Ching, "A tree as great as a man's embrace springs from a small shoot; a terrace nine stories high begins with a pile of earth; a journey of 1000 miles starts under one's feet."

Nothing can be completed unless it is first begun.

Today is the day to begin your journey and start your process. From the example of Abraham, it is clear that we will all struggle with doubt and the fear of the unknown as we begin our journey, yet it is still important that we act quickly to pursue the promise that God has for each of us.

Often times, life works according to seasons, and if we don't act with confidence and boldness without delay, we could find ourselves waiting for extended periods of time for the next season to arrive.

The faster that we do what God has called us to do, the faster we will receive the fulfillment of the promise.

For Meditation: What scriptures can you recall to mind when you're faced with… (a) feelings of worthlessness? (b) the tendency to procrastinate?

(Proverbs 6:6-9) **Go to the ant, thou sluggard; consider her ways, and be wise: Which having no guide, overseer, or ruler, Provideth her meat in the summer, and gathereth her food in the harvest. How long wilt thou sleep, O sluggard? when wilt thou arise out of thy sleep?** (KJV)

(Proverbs 24:30-34) **I passed by the field of one who was lazy, by the vineyard of a stupid person; and see, it was all overgrown with thorns; the ground was covered with nettles, and its stone wall was broken down. Then I saw and considered it; I looked and received instruction. A little sleep, a little slumber, a little folding of the hands to rest, and poverty will come upon you like a robber, and want, like an armed warrior.** (NRSV)

10

THE PROMISE DOES NOT REQUIRE PERFECTION

(Genesis 12:18) **So Pharaoh called Abram, and said, "What is this you have done to me? Why did you not tell me that she was your wife?**

(Genesis 12:19) **Why did you say, 'She is my sister,' so that I took her for my wife?** (NRSV)

We are created in the image of Greatness- only to be forgotten when we view ourselves in the mirror of doubt. -B.R.

F or so many years, I ran from my calling of preaching God's word. For years I struggled with the question of how God could use such an imperfect vessel like me to proclaim His perfect Word. Time after time, year after year, I refused to respond to the calling and promptings of God.

It was not until God allowed me to see the imperfections of others that He had called and was using mightily that my perspective changed. Only then did it become apparent that if God could use these imperfect people, He could surely use me too.

Accusations of Unworthiness

One of the greatest obstacles to the people of promise that keeps them from moving into their God-given purpose is the accusation by the enemy that tells us that we are unworthy. This tool has been used since the beginning of time to make us feel unworthy of our calling from God.

Paul spoke of these accusations of unworthiness by the enemy against the people of promise in Romans chapter 8. He assured us that God knows us full and well, including the areas where we fall short, but chose to save us anyway:

(Romans 8:29-31) **For those whom he foreknew he also predestined to be conformed to the image of his Son, in order that he might be the first-born among many brethren. And those whom he predestined he also called; and those whom he called he also justified; and those whom he justified he also glorified. What then shall we say to this? If God is for us, who is against us?** (RSV)

To make sure that we did not miss his point, Paul once again posed the question in verse 33 that he already answered in Verse 31:

(Romans 8:33) **Who will bring any charge against those whom God has chosen? It is God who justifies.** (NIV)

Remember, God has not called us to be perfect but to press toward the mark of His high calling. When we look at the word of

God, we find that God did some of His best work with the most imperfect people.

Noah abused alcohol.

Moses had anger issues.

David had wandering eyes.

Jonah was stubborn and unrepentant.

As a group, the disciples most likely would have failed most modern psychological examinations. Yes, even the bearer of the promise, Abraham, lied more than once. We can see this clear example in Scripture:

(Genesis 12:11) **And it came to pass, when he was come near to enter into Egypt, that he said unto Sarai his wife, Behold now, I know that thou art a fair woman to look upon...**

(Genesis 12:12) **Therefore it shall come to pass, when the Egyptians shall see thee, that they shall say, This is his wife: and they will kill me, but they will save thee alive.**

(Genesis 12:13) **Say, I pray thee, thou art my sister: that it may be well with me for thy sake; and my soul shall live because of thee.** (KJV)

Abraham was afraid of the repercussions of entering a foreign land with a beautiful wife. Instead of turning to God for an answer, he chose to protect himself by encouraging Sarah to lie and say that she was his sister instead of his wife.

God does His most perfect work with the most imperfect people.

Perfection: Daily we strive, yet never arrive

So many of us procrastinate and never begin our work because we doubt that we are adequately prepared. We constantly feel that we need more work in areas of our lives that we believe must be perfected before we can move forward with our promise and purpose. This is only our self-doubt talking; God has never required us to be perfect.

Throughout the Bible, in numerous cases, dysfunction did not mean disqualification. Often the more dysfunctional a person was, the greater their call and the greater the victory.

If perfection was necessary before something could be put to work, ideas would never be implemented. Products would never make it to the market. Top automotive, electronics and technological companies release products all the time, realizing that flaws are inevitable. If these companies waited for perfection, the market would change due to technological advancement and their marketing opportunity would have passed. Instead, they prepare to deal with these flaws later, as they are discovered, by releasing updated versions of the product instead of delaying a product launch altogether. As we pursue our promises, we should remember that perfection is not required. As our flaws are exposed, God's grace will "update" us to the necessary standard.

Additionally, we should always remember God's anointing and assignment for us is never annulled, cancelled or revoked. Consider, once we begin the process the enemy becomes more determined to deter us from our promise. Because we are then "moved up" on his watch list, we must expect more trials and temptations. So, just as perfection is not a pre-requisite to begin the process, you must remember that perfection is not required to continue the process. In other words, your promise is never cancelled because "you fall short of the mark." As Paul taught in Romans 8, no person or power may lay accusations against the elect of God because of the work done through Christ. Christ himself, desiring that we understand his purpose here on earth, and the scope of forgiveness and grace, stated in John 3:17, "For God sent not his Son into the world to condemn the world; but that the world through him might be saved." Whenever we fall short, Christ steps in and makes up the difference. Instead of counting our sins, Christ became accountable for them.

Finally, we must remember, even though we are forgiven in the "divine courts," we may still have to pay an earthly price or consequence for our sins. Although God may forgive us for stealing, the justice system may impose punishment should you be caught; God may forgive you for sex outside of its' intended context, but, an unplanned pregnancy may be the result of a few moments of uncontrolled emotions and careless actions. Just as there is no sin so great that cannot be covered by God's grace, there is no action performed that does not have a related consequence, whether realized (seen, felt, etc.) or not.

Take these Biblical examples to heart to relieve the burden of perfection when pursuing your purpose in life. No matter what people in your life have impressed upon you, God is not asking for you to be perfect. This call upon your life is about God's promise, God's purpose, and God's perfection to carry it out on your behalf.

Embrace the imperfections that make you human.

God has the power, ability, and desire to perform His most perfect work in the midst of your flaws and humanity to achieve His greater purpose for your life.

For Meditation: How does it make you feel when you ponder the imperfections of some of the great bible characters? What determination does this give you?

(1 John 3:20) **For if our heart condemn us, God is greater than our heart, and knoweth all things. (KJV)Psalm 103:13, 14) Like as a father pitieth [his] children, so the LORD pitieth them that fear him. For he knoweth our frame; he remembereth that we are dust.**

(1 John 1:9) **If we confess our sins, he is faithful and just to forgive us our sins, and to cleanse us from all unrighteousness.** (KJV)

11

THE PROMISE REQUIRES PARTICIPATION BUT NEVER MANIPULATION

(Genesis 16:2) **So Sarai said to Abram, "Now behold, the LORD has prevented me from bearing children. Please go in to my maid; perhaps I will obtain children through her." And Abram listened to the voice of Sarai.** (NAS95)

The Promise requires that you do all that you can humanly do, then, allow God to do all that he divinely does. -BR

One of our greatest human frailties is that we often view things through our limited human understanding. Because things do not move the way or in the timeframe that we desire, we often lose faith, or worse yet, decide to lend God a helping hand. Although losing faith is bad, lending a helping hand outside of His will is much worse.

We must remember that we were only given the Promise, NOT THE PLAN. Although we may be able to interpret God's intent, we can never fully understand or anticipate His actions.

Just as God told Isaiah, finite beings will never fully comprehend an infinite Creator:

(Isaiah 55:8) **For my thoughts are not your thoughts, neither are your ways my ways, saith the LORD.**

(Isaiah 55:9) **For as the heavens are higher than the earth, so are my ways higher than your ways, and my thoughts than your thoughts.** (KJV)

God's Master Plan

God devised a plan and set it into action long before we were conceived in thought or matter. Because of this, we are not privy to all that has happened before us or will happen after us. We can only see how things affect us at this particular time and place. God, in the beginning, devised a plan that would touch and affect the hearts of many, long after we have left this Earth.

As an example, we are simply the commuter awaiting the arrival of the train. The train has been scheduled by someone with much more information and a greater authority to influence the schedule and the corresponding behavior of the train. This person of authority has devised a strategic plan, having taken into consideration the needs of ALL commuters, the resources available, and other variables that we are not aware of.

The schedule has been made taking all of these things into consideration. As a result, and regardless of what we desire or think, the train will only arrive at its scheduled time. Whether we arrive five hours early or five minutes late, we cannot change the master schedule.

In the analogy above, it is very clear that the master, God, is in control. However, not as clear in the above example, is the all-important truth and guiding principle of any promise that God makes: we, too, have an obligation. We must show up in order to board the train- we must participate.

We Are Called to Participate

To participate is to join in, share, or collaborate. When we participate, we assume the role of co-creator, helper, facilitator, or assistant. It is not only God's design but His plan that we the people of promise would participate. Throughout the Scripture, we find that God calls us to participate.

Time and time again, after God gives His promise to His people, He then commands them to participate: "Go ye", "Bring ye", "Seek ye", "Come ye". Each of these phrases is simultaneously a command and an impassioned plea for each of us to do all that we humanly can while allowing God to do all that He will divinely do.

Promise manifestation requires YOUR participation.

Conversely, the act of manipulation is to usurp God's authority and attempt to take control, to force a particular outcome. When we seek to manipulate, it is because we have looked at the situation, considered the obstacles to be overcome, and decided that God is incapable of doing what He said, therefore, God requires our help. When we attempt to manipulate, we are saying much less about God and much more about ourselves.

When Sarah, who was well past the qualifying age of senior citizen, considered that her biological clock ran out of time many years before, she decided that God "needed" her help. Undoubtedly, she had never heard the old saying, "God never comes when you want Him, but He's always right on time."

Perhaps God's watch had stopped, or maybe He just didn't get the memo. For whatever reason, at that time, God had not provided what He had promised.

It is important for us to remember that any promise given by God will always move to an orchestrated end. The word "orchestrated" insinuates synchronized performance and harmonious melodies. These melodies can only be accomplished when each member of the orchestra plays their musical parts as directed by the conductor. To deviate from their parts, or to play without regard to the conductors directions, would result in nothing short of an "orchestrated mess".

Through Sarah's short sightedness and Abraham's passiveness, a centuries-old war has brewed among nations between the offspring of the illegitimate son Ishmael and God's promised child Isaac.

Sarah was unwilling to wait on the timing of God's promise since it didn't seem to be happening according to her perception of God's plan. Abraham was a guilty party since he allowed Sarah's deviation from God's plan to happen without resistance.

We Are God's Instruments

As God's people here on earth, we are His tools: His hands, feet, mouth, etc. For anything to be accomplished here on earth, God has to use us as His instruments. This can only happen if we make ourselves available. We must never become desperate and misbehave because of waning faith. We must always observe the proper parameters and not go outside of the lines of conduct.

In order for God's promise to be fulfilled, we will never be required to act contrary to God's will or his Word, as we saw in the example of Sarah and Abraham. Instead, we must trust that God can and will do exactly what He has promised; we are not responsible to make it happen in our own ability.

When we attempt to take the reins due to impatience or lack of faith in areas of our lives, we often derail God's plans. God has put in place a perfect plan before time began, and He will make good on His promises to us… if we only allow Him to.

For Meditation: Can you think of five reasons why God can better see the big picture than you can?

(Isaiah 6:8) **Also I heard the voice of the Lord, saying, Whom shall I send, and who will go for us? Then said I, Here am I; send me.**

(Philippians 2:13) **For it is God who works in you both to will and to do of His good pleasure.** (MKJV)

(1 Corinthians 3:8-9) **So he planting, and he watering, are one, and each one shall receive his own reward according to his own labor. For we are fellow-workers of God, a field of God, and you are a building of God.** (MKJV)

12

THE PROMISE IS NEVER WITHOUT PROBLEMS

(Genesis 12:10) **Now there was a famine in the land, and Abram went down to Egypt to live there for a while because the famine was severe.** (NIV)

Faith is the ability to look past what we see (the situation) and focus on where we are called to go (our destination). Never lose sight of your destination because you are pre-occupied with your situation...Stay in Faith!!! –BR

P roblems will propel you down the path to your promise. We often try to avoid problems at all cost, but many times, God will use problems to get us to the Land of our Promise. Yes, problems are a part of life. We are not exempt because of the promise; rather, problems are a pivotal key to receiving the promise.

Keep these foundational principles in mind on your journey to the promise:

Problems are essential to our promise. Just as time in the gym is necessary to increase your physical strength, problems are necessary to increase our spiritual strength in pursuit of the promise. Also, problems can be used as obstructions to either guide us to where God would have us go, or to keep us from traveling into hazardous areas. Problems can be positive.

The greater the promise, the greater the problems. We mistakenly believe that because we have a great call on our life that the way will be easy. A quick look at the life of Abraham reveals that the opposite is actually true. During sporting events like football or basketball, the opposing team will often "double team" a team's star player or a player that is considered a threat. In the same fashion, Satan goes to great extremes to stop those who are the greatest threat to his kingdom. If you possess a great promise, expect great resistance.

Problems are signs of progress toward the promise. In another football analogy, when a team is close to scoring, the opposing team shifts into a "red zone" defense, a special defense designed specifically to keep the team from scoring in short-yardage situations. When the problems and their intensity increase, it could be that you are much closer to success than you know.

Because Abraham was doing what God had ordered, one would assume that the process would have been smooth sailing. Abraham had been directed to a foreign land, and suddenly, he faced a famine. Our natural reaction is to think that the problem was to keep Abraham from his promise, however, it appeared that the famine was actually used to direct Abraham to the portion of his promise in the land of Egypt.

When we look at Genesis 12:16, we find that Abraham was treated well by Pharaoh and increased in riches:

(Genesis 12:16) **And for her (Sarai) sake he dealt well with Abram; and he had sheep, oxen, male donkeys, male and female slaves, female donkeys, and camels.** (NRSV)

Although his stay in Egypt resulted in great financial gain, Abraham's journey to the promise was not without numerous other problems. Here is a brief list of some of the many problems that Abraham encountered along the way:

1. The land endured a famine.

2. Abraham went to Egypt and feared for his life.

3. Eventually, Abraham and those around him became so blessed that they encountered more problems maintaining their possessions.

4. As a result of those promises, Abraham was forced to split from his nephew Lot.

5. Lot was then captured by a large military force, and Abraham assembled all of his servants to go save Lot.

6. Abraham's wife could not have children.

7. Abraham listened to his wife and took Hagar the servant, resulting in an illegitimate child not ordered by God.

8. Abraham listened to his wife and sent Hagar away, thereby losing his son Ishmael.

9. God gave Abraham the fulfillment of his promise, only to ask him to sacrifice his child Isaac.

As God moves us to a new location, He has to get our attention, which often requires making us uncomfortable in the process. This was the case with the stories in the Bible of Elijah at the brook and Jonah in the belly of the whale. Both of these great men of God were made incredibly uncomfortable so that they might receive the promise God had for them. Both were willing to proceed, only after problems arose forcing them along the way.

Do you recall the story of Elijah? After Elijah informed King Ahab that there would be a drought in the land, God ordered Eljah to flee to the brook Cherith. God had arranged for Elijah to live there in exile, drinking from his own private oasis while the ravens delivered food for him twice a day. Elijah's obedience caused God to provide a private sanctuary for him while the other inhabitants of the land suffered through a famine. It stands to reason that Elijah enjoyed a comfortable existence there, sipping from his own private pool and enjoying his own private "meals on wings" food service. Unfortunately, comfort can be the enemy of progress because it lulls us into a state of complacency. As a fact of the matter, progress is most often accompanied by discomfort. Because God desired to move Elijah to the town of Zarephath, where a widow and her son were preparing their last bit of food before they made ready to die, God had to make Elijah's existence uncomfortable with problems; the brook dried up and the raven stopped flying. Because his source had dried up, Elijah was forced to move to another location, thereby, allowing him to move to his next level of purpose to provide the widow and her son, as well as himself with a never ending barrel of meal and cruse of oil (1 Kings 17).

Problems Can Be Self-Inflicted

To qualify, there are many times that problems in our lives are self-inflicted and are not caused by God. If we are buying things that we can't afford, entering into relationships with people that we know are wrong for us, or directly going against the commandments of God, then we are bound to have problems in our lives.

While attaining the promise that God has for you does not require you to be perfect by any means, it is important that you are following God's instructions for our lives to avoid many unnecessary problems and self-inflicted heartaches.

Once you know that you are on the path to God's promise for you, know that there will be problems that arise. The journey to the promise is not guaranteed to be smooth; it will be bumpy and have obstacles along the way. Yet we can be encouraged in the fact that these problems are a part of life as we pursue the promise. Even the greatest men of faith in the Bible faced numerous problems on their journey to receive God's promise for them.

For Meditation: Why is faith needed to deal with necessary problems now? Why would it be unreasonable to expect a life without problems now?

(John 16:33) **These things I have spoken unto you, that in me ye might have peace. In the world ye shall have tribulation: but be of good cheer; I have overcome the world.** (KJV)

(Psalms 34:19) **A righteous man may have many troubles, but the LORD delivers him from them all;** (NIV)

(Matthew 5:10, 11) **Blessed are they which are persecuted for righteousness' sake: for theirs is the kingdom of heaven. Blessed are ye, when men shall revile you, and persecute you, and shall say all manner of evil against you falsely, for my sake.**

13

THE PROMISE REQUIRES PATIENCE

(Genesis 12:4) **So Abram went forth as the LORD had spoken to him; and Lot went with him. Now Abram was seventy-five years old when he departed from Haran.** (NASB)

(Genesis 21:5) **Now Abraham was one hundred years old when his son Isaac was born to him.** (NASB)

There are some problems in life we can work out...but there are some problems in life that we can only wait out. -BR

W aiting or "wilderness" periods are essential in the ongoing process of your promise. It is our natural inclination to avoid these times of our lives at all cost. However, there is crucial preparation that occurs during these periods. Although the transformation may not be obvious, like that of the larvae that endures the cocoon before emerging as a butterfly, so do these periods prepare us for the next level of our lives.

A popular rock song from years ago stated accurately, "The waiting is the hardest part." To wait would imply that it is a passive activity, requiring no effort. However, even the youngest children realize that waiting requires great effort and internal strength. Waiting requires patience.

Patience is considered a virtue, a character trait to be desired and treasured. Patience is further defined as a quiet, steady perseverance; diligence; even-tempered care. This trait can only be cultivated through the process of waiting.

The writer of Hebrews clearly stated that the reason Abraham received the promise was because he waited for the promise. The world is full of sad and depressing stories of gifted individuals skilled in business, education, and other areas that possessed creative genius, amazing abilities, great dreams, and an above-average desire to succeed. Unfortunately, these same individuals often gave up just before their dreams were realized.

Patience Is Required to Receive the Promise

Few Christians understand the connection between the promise given and the patience required. The Bible is littered with stories about chosen people who experienced delays in receiving their promise.

Daniel, an extraordinary man of God who understood the connection between faith and prayer, experienced a delay that Christians often experience while waiting on the promise. In Daniel 10:4, after praying and fasting for three full weeks, Daniel was greeted by an angel that explained how he had been dispatched from heaven the moment that Daniel began to pray but had been assaulted and delayed in the heavens by one of Satan's Angels. If Daniel, a devout man of prayer and fasting, would be subject to waiting for an answer, what does that say about any normal believer who lives today surrounded by a world of sin?

Amazingly enough, Jesus, the ultimate Promise given by the Promise Giver Himself, knew what it was like to wait. Jesus, the perfect Son of God, waited and endured thirty years of relative obscurity, only to burst forth at the appointed time to transform the world and its view of God and religion, within a relatively short ministry career of only three years.

Jesus spent 90% of His time here on earth waiting, and only 10% doing what He had been sent here to do.

As the old saying goes, all good things take time. Such is the case, even with the things of God. One would think that the promise given to Abraham to birth His chosen nation, the foundation for God's people and His Holy Word, would have gotten expedited service. We would assume that this project would have been implemented and completed quickly, fast, and in a hurry.

Abraham was given the promise at the age of 75, after which he wandered from place to place for 25 years awaiting the manifestation of that promise. The promise, as important as it was, was not fulfilled until Abraham was 100 years old. As you pursue your promise, never grow discouraged. It is clear, that even the chosen of God have to wait.

God's Unique Timing

It is hard to imagine that the One who holds time in His hand, the One who was in the beginning and will be at the end, appears to be confined by time. Here we must establish that God's view of time is completely different from our view of time. Because our lives are finite, we view time in that manner within the limited scope of our lives.

The writer of Psalms in 144:4 (RSV) compared human life to a breath and a fleeting shadow; in Psalms 39:5, the writer arrived at the conclusion that his lifetime was nothing in the sight of God.

But God on the other hand, is omnipresent and eternal, stretching from before time began until long after the final bell has rung. 2 Peter 3:8 declares to us, "That one day is with the Lord as a thousand years, and a thousand years as one day." Someone once said that time waits for no man. Because God controls time, He never waits.

Since God uses time as he sees fit, he appears as a long-term strategic planner. He is not just concerned with today but a thousand years from today. He is not just concerned with how something affects you and your children but equally concerned with how it affects your children's children and beyond.

God's Time versus Our Time

You have probably heard people say, "It's up to God, and it will happen in His time." This statement is only partially true. Just as we learned that the promise requires our participation, it is also important to remember that there are some things we must do to allow God to proceed with His plan.

There are two aspects of time: Our time and God's time.

In our time, we have all control and are responsible for using it properly. In God's time, we have no responsibility or control since He has the final say. To understand the concept of our time and God's time, consider the following example:

In our time, we must seize the opportunity and move forward with great urgency.

There is a single mother struggling to make ends meet. She already holds a steady position at her company, yet she so desperately needs a promotion. She prays for a new job and believes that God has answered her prayer. In her spirit, she knows that God has promised her a new job. Here is where most people fail: They have heard from God, yet think that they need to do nothing at all.

Remember, God requires our participation.

In this situation, the single mother must do her part and assist the situation along. With urgency, she must begin the process by checking job openings and listings. She must find out the minimum job requirements and immediately begin securing those credentials.

She must determine what specific classes she must take to earn the right credentials and qualifications for a new job. These are all things that the single mother must do since she is in charge of her time.

The process of the promise cannot progress until she prepares for her opportunity.

In God's time, we have no control, and it is totally up to Him. God's promises are always preceded by God's preparation, the things that occur behind the scenes, much of which we never see.

To fulfill the promise to the single mother, God begins to prepare the way. He may do this by touching the heart of someone in that position that the single mother desires, creating in them a desire to move to another city or state so that they might be closer to family. Or perhaps, God touches the management team at a company where the single mother decides to apply so that they determine that the workload is too great for that department, deciding to open another slot.

Here the single mother has no control, but God has it all.

A good friend of mine, Bud Orrell, loves to say, "Your blessing is on the way, but because God wants you to have His best, it takes a little time for God to get it ready."

Is the thought that God takes time to prepare certain situations or outcomes that preposterous? Not really when you take into account that God's promises are specific to each person. Think about the fact that God has to bring the recipient of a particular promise into contact with the right person, out of the billions of people in this world, who possesses the very thing necessary to fulfill the promise. Even more, he has to direct us to certain people and places while allowing us to operate with the freedom of choice. Wow, It's a wonder he get's anything accomplished!!

As God prepared the people of the promise, the descendants of Abraham, to move into the Promised Land, He reminded them what a great blessing lay before them:

(Deuteronomy 6:10) **When the LORD your God brings you into the land he swore to your fathers, to Abraham, Isaac and Jacob, to give you-- a land with large, flourishing cities you did not build,**

(Deuteronomy 6:11) **houses filled with all kinds of good things you did not provide, wells you did not dig, and vineyards**

and olive groves you did not plant-- then when you eat and are satisfied. (NIV)

For God to fulfill the promise to the children of Israel, to give them a blessing beyond anything that they could imagine, it took time. God had to allow the enemies of Israel the time to design the cities, to build houses, to fill those houses with all manner of good things, to plant gardens and vineyards, and to supply all the necessities to provide an abundant life for those to whom He had made the promise. A life that was far above any they could have imagined.

God Prepares for Our Promise

In our lives, God prepares for our promise, but we must allow time for others to design, build, plant, shape, create, manufacture, develop, and even maintain those things that God desires to give to us... until we too have been prepared to receive the blessings that God has for us.

If we can fully develop the virtue of waiting, perhaps it will be said of us that we, just like our father Abraham, have patiently waited and obtained the promise:

(Hebrews 6:15) **And so, having patiently waited, he obtained the promise.** (NAS95)

Yes, it may take longer than we think it should, but God is working according to His master schedule and not our own. More importantly, the reason that it takes time is because God is rearranging things and making moves like a great chess player in the sky. He is maneuvering us and the right people and things that we need to meet in the right place at the right time. Additionally, there are thousands and thousands of other promises in other lives that are linked to ours. As God works to prepare and deliver our blessings to us, He is also using US to help fulfill the promises in the lives of others. God is working behind the scenes to give us not only what we need when we need it, but to fully equip us so that we WILL obtain our promise.

For Meditation: Why must we be patient when waiting for God's blessing at times?

(Romans 5:3-4) **And not only so, but we glory in tribulations also: knowing that tribulation worketh patience; And patience, experience; and experience, hope:** (KJV)

(James 5:7) **Be patient therefore, brethren, unto the coming of the Lord. Behold, the husbandman waiteth for the precious fruit of the earth, and hath long patience for it, until he receive the early and latter rain.**

14

THE PROMISE REQUIRES PERSEVERANCE

(Genesis 22:1) **And it happened after these things that God tested Abraham...** (MKJV)

As you travel on path of your Promise, never be discouraged because the obstacles ahead of you seem to get larger. They do, because you're getting closer to them. This is the way it MUST BE!! To overcome them, you must stand face to face, get right up close so that you can analyze it, dissect it, and figure it out. Only when you're that close will you discover that you, and the gifts you have been blessed with, are MUCH LARGER than what you face. God allows obstacles in our life, not to be feared, but to be OVERCOME!!! -BR

A ny great baseball player will tell you that striking out is part of the game. Even the most celebrated players only hit the ball about three out of every ten times. This means every time they approach the plate, there is a 70 percent chance of failure. However, these players understand that in order to get on base, they have to keep swinging the bat. In the same manner, the Promise requires that you continue to pursue in spite of challenges, trials, setbacks and disappointments because failure is never final, unless you fail to try.

Throughout the Bible, faith is used synonymously with patience; patience is often used interchangeably with perseverance. In the book of Hebrews, perseverance is used to describe a person's ability to wait. Perseverance, or endurance, describes one's ability to continue in spite of difficulty, discouragement, opposition, or trials.

(Hebrews 10:36) **You need to persevere so that when you have done the will of God, you will receive what he has promised.** (NIV)

(Hebrews 10:36) **For you need endurance, so that when you have done the will of God, you may receive what was promised.** (NRSV)

This perseverance speaks of the ability, mindset, and tenacity to endure the problem.

Many times, we fail to see that opposition and problems, although not always, can be tools used by God to lead us and keep us on track to the promise. Only by enduring the challenges will we be able to possess what has been promised to us.

Write the Vision

The prophet Habakkuk was given a damning and devastating prophecy regarding the future of the Jewish people. God would allow the Chaldeans to brutally oppress the Jews so that He might try the faith and patience of His people. After distinguishing between the hypocrites and the sincere among them, He would then repay the Chaldeans for their sins against Him.

God instructed Habakkuk to "write the vision, and make it plain." Basically, write the details of the prophecy God had given as legibly as possible, stated in plain and simple language on stone tablets, so that it would be easily understood by all who read it through the ages.

God then reassured Habakkuk that the revelation given to him was for a specific reason and would come to pass. Habakkuk 2:3 (NASB) says, "For the vision is yet for the appointed time; it hastens toward the goal, and it will not fail. Though it tarries, wait for it; for it will certainly come, it will not delay."

Do Not Forget the Promise

God assures Habakkuk that because the promise would not happen for some time, the details must be written, so that it would not be forgotten. The vision, or His word and what He had promised, would manifest at an appointed time; a time that was determined and known by God alone. It shall speak, or be fully accomplished, and not disputed.

Although it would take considerable time from the prophet's hearing of the promise to its fulfillment, the promise would happen exactly when it was supposed to. Only then would the Chaldeans be made to pay for their transgressions against God. Until the time that God determined, the chosen people of God would have to endure.

Perseverance is required from all that travel the road to Promise.

Abraham, after departing from his home in faith, encountered a famine in Genesis 12:10. God used this famine to direct the recipient of His promise to Egypt. In Egypt, because of his beautiful wife, Abraham feared for his life and asked Sarah to lie about her identity.

Just as Abraham had feared, Pharaoh, after hearing of Sarah's beauty, took her to be one of the royal court. Because of Sarah, Pharaoh was kind to Abraham by giving him sheep, male and female oxen, camels, and servants, both male and female.

However, because of His divine promise and plan, God plagued the house of Pharaoh so that he eventually begged Abraham to take his wife back and to get out of town in a hurry. Instead of losing his life, as Abraham had feared, God turned this problem into a lucrative payday of the promise, and Abraham left Egypt a very rich man.

For every problem, there is a blessing proportionate to the difficulty of the problem.

So many of us want a picture of what we have to gain to keep us inspired when times get hard. For Abraham, a glimpse of the reward was only gained after the journey was well underway. We too must be like Abraham to persevere, willing to endure even without concrete evidence of the promise that we are pursuing.

Caleb and Joshua are other wonderful examples of perseverance in the Bible:

(Numbers 13:30) **And Caleb stilled the people before Moses, and said, Let us go up at once, and possess it; for we are well able to overcome it.**

We Must Possess

It must be our mindset to possess our Promise, like our biblical forefathers, Abraham, Caleb, and Joshua. For them, there was no obstacle too great or people too strong. No mountain was too high to keep them from the promise that lay before them.

Sometimes it must be enough to hold on to the report of "the goodness" of the land. That report should be enough to encourage us to move forward. So many people are too busy focusing on the negatives that they can't see the blessings before them; they are unable to let go of the bad report to continue on to pursue the promise.

Let nothing stop you from possessing what God has for you. Perseverance is a key component to receiving the promise, and our endurance on our journey is always met with a sure reward.

For Meditation: What in your life causes you to need perseverance most? How can you endure?

(James 1:2-4) **My brothers and sisters, whenever you face trials of any kind, consider it nothing but joy, because you know that the testing of your faith produces endurance; and let endurance have its full effect, so that you may be mature and complete, lacking in nothing.** (NRSV)

(Matthew 24:13) **But the one who endures to the end will be saved.** (NRSV)

(Galatians 6:9) **So let us not grow weary in doing what is right, for we will reap at harvest-time, if we do not give up.** (NRSV)

15

THE PROMISE IS PROGRESSIVE AND REVEALED PIECE BY PIECE

(Hebrews 11:8) **By faith Abraham obeyed when he was called to set out for a place that he was to receive as an inheritance; and he set out, not knowing where he was going.** (NRSV)

How do we know what path to follow as we travel on the journey to Purpose? It is not the road that offers the fewest obstacles, the safest passage or even a definite destination, but, it is the one that awakens and calls to something within us; for a failure to answer the call results in a failure to live. -BR

As humans, we naturally want to know the end from the beginning. Yet this is not the way that God works. We must move forward in faith from one milestone to the next in order for God to give further directions for the next phase of the journey.

In Robert Frost's poem, The Road Less Traveled, it recants the agonizing decision endured as he tried to decide which fork in the road he would take:

Robert Frost (1874–1963). Mountain Interval. 1920.
1. The Road Not Taken

TWO roads diverged in a yellow wood,
And sorry I could not travel both
And be one traveler, long I stood
And looked down one as far as I could
To where it bent in the undergrowth;

Then took the other, as just as fair,
And having perhaps the better claim,
Because it was grassy and wanted wear;
Though as for that the passing there
Had worn them really about the same,

And both that morning equally lay
In leaves no step had trodden black.
Oh, I kept the first for another day!
Yet knowing how way leads on to way,
I doubted if I should ever come back.

I shall be telling this with a sigh
Somewhere ages and ages hence:
Two roads diverged in a wood, and I—
I took the one less traveled by,
And that has made all the difference.

By choosing the road less traveled, Frost declares that his decision actually made his life better. Because of his decision, he was able to see and experience things that no one else had. Instead of becoming a "rank and file" follower, he became a leader and visionary- which is a rare find in the world of today. Instead of simply blending in with the masses, he took his own unique journey through life, showing us that a place at the front of the pack will always afford a better view.

Although Frost expressed regret for not being able to travel both paths, he should be applauded for taking action, making a decision and beginning the journey. Unfortunately, many of us, when faced with a decision, are paralyzed with fear and doubt and never choose to begin the journey at all. To choose one fork over the other is to consciously decide that you must forego what lies at the end of one path to experience what lies at the end of the other. It is unfortunate that we can't experience both, but a fact of life, and a reliable indicator of a person's maturity, is realizing that every decision carries with it a certain amount of risk. Throughout history, those who have made the greatest contributions to society have been those who have chosen to follow a path with no guarantee as to where it might lead - they took risks.

It is the fear of making the wrong decision or journeying down the wrong road that grips so many of these people that never even begin their journey, they never pursue their dreams. Ironically, by not consciously making a choice, they are unconsciously making the choice to live a life that is inferior to what God desires for them.

This brings us to the topic of regret. It is very rare, if not impossible for any of us to go through life without a single regret. According to an NIH Public Access publication, regret additionally has a number of cognitive side effects, such as increased blame, superstition, suspicion, and disappointment. This regret is often characterized as a negative emotion due to a person feeling fault in an action that they had taken and should have done differently. According to this research, the six biggest regrets of Americans are education, career, romance, parenting, self-improvement, and leisure, according to the figures on the following page.

As people enter the later years of their life, they are often plagued with regret for never gathering the courage to move forward and live their lives without fear and timidity. This can include all areas of life, including love, business, and risks or new opportunities. You are probably familiar with the famous quote by Alfred Lord Tennyson, "Tis better to have loved and lost than never to have loved at all." This is the exact attitude people must have in relationships, work, and their personal choices to occasionally say, "Why not? What do I have to lose!"

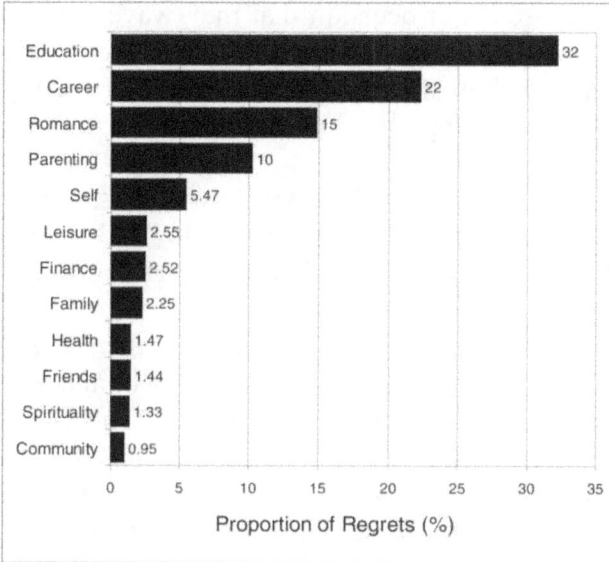

So many of these people never even begin their journey for fear that they will journey down the wrong road. Dreams denied, lives not lived, the failure to live from fear to live. Still, we must never forget that mistakes are temporary, but regrets last for a lifetime.

Today, many people never begin anything because of fear. This especially holds true for Christians who spend most of their time asking themselves, "Is this what God would have me to do?" They become so paralyzed with the fear of doing something that is displeasing to God that they never do anything. This is called "paralysis by analysis", where we are gripped by fear and forced into indecision.

Dr. Myles Munroe says that the richest place on the face of the Earth is the graveyard because there you'll find a wealth of ideas, dreams, and possibilities that were buried along with the person that God had given them to without ever coming to fruition. These ideas, inventions, and ideologies were given by God to be a blessing to and through his promised people but were miscarried or stillborn and died before seeing life.

Ideas that are never initiated represent investments by God that never benefited the kingdom as intended.

Equally guilty are the people that begin a good work with great zeal and intensity, but falter when they come to a crossroads. It is here at the crossroads of decision that they waver, awaiting some mystical direction from God, paralyzed with fear of making the wrong decision, so they make no decision. Not realizing that by sheer virtue of not deciding, they are murdering the promise that lies deep within.

When you find yourself at this crossroads, remember the words of a wise old preacher, "It's easier to lead a mule that is moving than it is to lead one that is standing still." Just do something!

There are two types of fear spoken of in the Bible, one good and one bad. The good fear is based upon respect and appreciation for the Commandments and instructions of God. This type of fear is beneficial and life-giving, one that enhances our life. The Bible speaks of this fear in many ways:

(Proverbs 1:7) **The fear of the LORD is the beginning of knowledge: but fools despise wisdom and instruction.** (KJV)

(Proverbs 9:10) **The fear of the LORD is the beginning of wisdom: and the knowledge of the holy is understanding.**

(Proverbs 22:4) **The reward of humility and the fear of the LORD are riches, honor and life.** (NAS95)

(Psalms 33:8) **Let all the earth fear the LORD: let all the inhabitants of the world stand in awe of him.**

(Proverbs 15:16) **Better is a little with the fear of the LORD than great treasure and trouble with it.** (RSV)

The other type of fear is ungodly and detrimental to ourselves and those around us. This is the fear of people, fear of what those people say about us, fear of the world, fear of circumstances, even fear of the unknown. This type of fear manifests in many different forms: stress, worry, anxiety, sleeplessness, depression, and uneasiness; call it what you want, they are all some sort of fear.

Today in these times of financial uncertainty, in times of home foreclosures and bank defaults, many are afraid to move to the right or the left. We attempt to just mark time for fear of making the wrong decision. That is why God insisted that we not become attached to the things of this world because fear is oppression.

Yet if we must trust and believe that God has our best interest at heart, Hebrews 13:5-6 says, "Keep your lives free from the love of money and be content with what you have, because God has said, 'Never will I leave you; never will I forsake you.' So we say with confidence, 'The Lord is my helper; I will not be afraid. What can man do to me?'" (NIV)

(Matthew 6:19) **Lay not up for yourselves treasures upon earth, where moth and rust doth corrupt, and where thieves break through and steal:**

(Matthew 6:20) **But lay up for yourselves treasures in heaven, where neither moth nor rust doth corrupt, and where thieves do not break through nor steal.** (KJV)

Fear strangles us and takes us captive.

Proverbs 29:25 (MKJV) says, "The fear of man brings a snare, but whoever puts his trust in the LORD shall be safe." Fear causes us to act in opposition to what God desires. Faith encourages, and fear discourages. Faith commands us to trust the promises of God, while fear causes to doubt that any good thing can happen.

David, one of the most courageous men ever, said in Psalms 27:1, "The LORD is my light and my salvation; whom shall I fear? The LORD is the strength of my life; of whom shall I be afraid?" David understood that on the path to promise there is no room for fear, and as long as the Lord was on his side, no person or thing could stop him.

Throughout the Bible, as Jesus went about the countryside, he preached to those he encountered "fear not" because there was no problem that was too great. No situation, no circumstance, no sickness or condition was or ever would be beyond His control.

In Matthew 10:28, Jesus even went as far as instructing believers to not be afraid of the one thing that was considered final, death of the body. After the ruler of the synagogue, Jairus, was told his daughter was dead in Luke chapter 8, Jesus comforts Jairus, "Don't be afraid; just believe, and she will be healed." Upon entering Jairus's home, Jesus announced to those present that the young girl was not dead, but merely asleep. Those who had gathered to mourn her death ridiculed Jesus because they knew she was not breathing; but, they did not know the power that Jesus possessed. After taking her by the hand and telling her to "get up", life entered her body once again. Jesus repeated the miracle in raising Lazarus and eventually in being raised from the dead himself. He proved that nothing, not even death, was beyond the power of the kingdom.

Finally, Timothy reminds us that we were created as perfect creatures, and fear is not a part of us.

(2Timothy 1:7) **For God hath not given us the spirit of fear; but of power, and of love, and of a sound mind.**

Fear is merely a tool of the enemy, False Evidence Appearing Real - a thought placed in our mind by the enemy to confuse and discourage us from completing the task that we were sent forth to do. Therefore, we follow the advice of the Apostle Paul in 2 Corinthians 10:5 "Casting down imaginations, and every high thing that exalteth itself against the knowledge of God, and bringing into captivity every thought to the obedience of Christ".

In other words, you must never allow your fears of "what might happen" to prevent anything from happening. This is the truth we all must embrace to prevent the paralysis of fear that results in indecision. If we want any hope of eliminating regret, seizing opportunities that God places in our path, and living up to our fullest potential, it is essential to cast down fear and embrace the knowledge of God.

This is the key that will eliminate a life of regret and allow us to take advantage of every opportunity in our path as we journey along the road less traveled…

For Meditation: How have you allowed fear and uncertainty to control your life before? What is you determination now?

(Proverbs 3:6) **In all thy ways acknowledge him, and he shall direct thy paths.** (KJV)

(Proverbs 16:9) **The human mind plans the way, but the LORD directs the steps.** (NRSV)

(Isaiah 30:21) **And when you turn to the right or when you turn to the left, your ears shall hear a word behind you, saying, "This is the way; walk in it."** (NRSV)

(Proverbs 4:18) **But the path of the just is as the shining light, that shineth more and more unto the perfect day.**

16

THE PRICE OF THE PROMISE IS PERSONAL SACRIFICE

(Genesis 22:2) **Then God said, "Take your son, your only son, Isaac, whom you love, and go to the region of Moriah. Sacrifice him there as a burnt offering on one of the mountains I will tell you about."** (NIV)

For anything worth having one must pay the price; and the price is always work, patience, love, self-sacrifice - no paper currency, no promises to pay, but the gold of real service. -John Burroughs

A s you pursue the promise, it is human nature to worry about what you might lose in the process. However, the better question is, "What do you stand to gain?"

There is a universal spiritual law that states "nothing can be gained without something first being given." It has been stated many ways, but the Bible states in Galatians 6:7, "whatever a person sows (gives or plants), that shall he also reap (get or harvest)." Actually, we can expand on that truth; as we discussed in Chapter 6 regarding Profit, any spiritual investment will always yield a much greater return.

What you give up will always pale in comparison to the fulfillment of the promise in your life.

Many potentially great people have lived lives that were mired in normalcy, and confined by conventionality, because they succumbed to their fear of loss. Others, who were designed for uncommon purpose, will never experience their destiny because they are unwilling to sacrifice something, anything, today, for a greater tomorrow.

Although the example of Abraham sacrificing his son Isaac is an extreme instance, the principles of his actions offer a great example of true sacrifice. The definition of sacrifice is: to forfeit something highly valued for the sake of one considered to have a greater value or claim. Simply put, one must "give freely to receive liberally." Although this concept appears easy to comprehend, realistically, it is difficult to grasp because of the human ego.

Ego can be identified as the culprit or source of all of our individual, and most, if not all of the world's collective offenses and misfortunes. It is ego that fuels the deadly sins of lust, greed, pride, and anger, which are the catalyst to quarrel and conflict. To possess a true spirit of sacrifice, one must crucify the ego that controls us.

From the life of Abraham we find two things necessary to crucify the ego that resides in each of us. As a preface, the term used in killing the ego; "crucify" is an appropriate term because it denotes a slow painful process full of torment. The slaying of one's ego is nothing short of that.

Firstly, to overcome ego, you must understand that anything that you can hold, touch or handle is only temporary. Regardless of the designer label or exclusive tag, even the best garments will eventually wear out; no matter how shiny and beautiful that new car is, eventually it will wind up as scrap metal; no matter how beautiful and well-built your dream home, it too will rot and decay. All "things" are temporary, and will come to an end.

A form of ego that stands between us and a life of promise is a "scarcity" mentality. As we seek to fulfill the calling of our life, we struggle with letting go of things...things that we have tricked ourselves into thinking that we need, but actually provide no true fulfillment in our lives.

In the story of the rich young ruler in Matthew 19, we see a young man that was unfulfilled amidst all of his wealth and earthly possessions. If his life had been so good because of his riches, then why was he not content; why was he still in search of fulfillment?

Matthew 19:16 **And, behold, one came and said unto him, Good Master, what good thing shall I do, that I may have eternal life?**

(17) And he said unto him, Why callest thou me good? there is none good but one, that is, God: but if thou wilt enter into life, keep the commandments.

(18) He saith unto him, Which? Jesus said, Thou shalt do no murder, Thou shalt not commit adultery, Thou shalt not steal, Thou shalt not bear false witness,

(19) Honour thy father and thy mother: and, Thou shalt love thy neighbour as thyself.

(20) The young man saith unto him, All these things have I kept from my youth up: what lack I yet?

(21) Jesus said unto him, If thou wilt be perfect, go and sell that thou hast, and give to the poor, and thou shalt have treasure in heaven: and come and follow me.

(22) But when the young man heard that saying, he went away sorrowful: for he had great possessions.

(23) Then said Jesus unto his disciples, Verily I say unto you, That a rich man shall hardly enter into the kingdom of heaven. (KJV)

Through this parable, we find Abraham's second revelation on sacrifice. The young ruler had given his power to his possessions, but, the great reality of the Promise is this: The things of our life are given to be a blessing, never a burden. Abraham realized that everything he had was a gift from God anyway…if God wants it he CAN take it at any time. If you can grab this one truth, living a life of Promise becomes infinitely easier. Ego, lulls us into believing that what we have is due to who we are rather than whose we are. Because Abraham understood that God has the final word on ALL matters, it was easy for him to let go and LET GOD.

A Life of Sacrifice

Had Abraham never begun the process, he would likely never have left his hometown, or maybe even his own neighborhood for that matter. Here, it is important to note, had Abraham not left to pursue the promise, the promise might have been delayed, but it would not have been canceled. God would have been forced to utilize someone else.

As Abraham pursued the promise and changed his life, there was the great risk of failure. What if he moved to a land that he had never visited before, only to have to return home with his tail between his legs? As Moses pursued God's promise, there was a risk of death as Pharaoh chased him and his people out of Egypt.

These great men of the Bible felt the same pressure that you and I feel today as we are called to pursue God's great promise that lies before us. The process of the promise is never easy; it does require sacrifice and may pose a risk to the things that you hold dear in your life.

Yet this sacrifice is never without a great and long-lasting reward, given to us directly by God as we attain the promised blessings that He has in store for us. We must always remember that we did nothing to qualify ourselves, but rather, God pre-qualified us before time began. Although we were chosen, we must prepare ourselves to sacrifice those things that are not vital to our promise. When the time for sacrifice arrives, don't just ask what you have to lose, but also, what you stand to gain …

We sacrifice fear for faith.
We sacrifice conflict for contentment.
We sacrifice frustration for fulfillment.
We sacrifice mediocrity for greatness.

For Meditation: What are you willing to sacrifice for God's promise to you?

(Luke 9:23) **And he said to them all, If any man will come after me, let him deny himself,**

(Luke 18:29-30) **And he said unto them, Verily I say unto you, There is no man that hath left house, or parents, or brethren, or wife, or children, for the kingdom of God's sake, Who shall not receive manifold more in this present time, and in the world to come life everlasting.** (KJV)

17

THE PROMISE NEVER NEGATES THE NEED FOR PREPARATION

(Genesis 14:14) **And when Abram heard that his relative had been taken captive, he led out his trained men, born in his house, three hundred and eighteen, and went in pursuit as far as Dan.** (NASB)

Plan before beginning...
Prepare before necessary...
Produce when given the opportunity...
-B.R.

W e often mistakenly believe that because we are the Promise Bearers, it negates our need to make preparation. We think that because God said we will receive the promise, we are off the hook. To many people, this implies an exception to the normal duties of one's calling.

Although given the promise from God Himself, we are still obligated to plan and prepare for unforeseen circumstances. Just like we must "participate", it is also our responsibility to do all that we possibly can to be the best that we can be. God will take over in areas that we can't humanly control, but we must hold up our end of the bargain.

To guarantee your success, prepare like it's totally dependent upon you, then pray like it's totally dependent upon God.

There is an old saying you may be familiar with: "When you fail to plan, you unintentionally plan to fail." Although Abraham was chosen to receive the promise, he took time to prepare and train his servants for war before there was even a threat. He did not assume that just because he was chosen for a mission by God that he would be insulated from the circumstances of life:

(Genesis 14:14) **When Abram heard that his relative had been taken captive, he led out his trained men, born in his house, three hundred and eighteen, and went in pursuit as far as Dan.** (NAS95)

As Jesus stated in Matthew 5:45 (NIV), "He causes his sun to rise on the evil and the good, and sends rain on the righteous and the unrighteous." Conversely, we can assume that the old saying is correct, "In every life, a little rain must fall."

As it says in Ecclesiastes:

(Ecclesiastes 9:11) **I again saw under the sun that the race is not to the swift, and the battle is not to the warriors, and neither is bread to the wise, nor wealth to the discerning, nor favor to men of ability; for time and chance overtake them all.** (NASB)

Expect a Great Attack

The greater that the calling on your life is - and the greater the promise that you have been given - the greater attack that you can expect. We can once again consider Job chapter 1. Job was a great servant of God under an even greater attack due to the promise that God had for his life.

When the Angels of the Lord assembled before God, Satan was present in the assembly. God inquired of Satan, "Where have you been, and what have you been doing?" Satan replied that he had been traveling throughout the world, looking for an opportunity to tempt men. Amazingly, God then suggested that the devil turn his attention toward Job because of his unwavering faith and dedication. For whatever reason, Job's dedication and loyalty - things that earned him a distinguished honor - also earned him the full attack of the enemy.

In Genesis 14:14, Abraham, after learning of the attack and capture of his nephew Lot, gathered together 318 trained servants that served under his rule. It is important to note that these were not mercenaries that fought for money, but rather, men that fought under the flag and faith of Abraham. These were men that had been born in the servitude of Abraham.

Although their duties included tending to necessary chores for such a large estate, like the household and livestock that required plenty of work, Abraham deliberately took time to prepare his servants for unforeseen occurrences. The servants were instructed, trained, and drilled to fend off a possible attack.

Abraham understood that even though he was promised, he must still prepare for possible problems.

Expect the Unexpected

By preparing for the unexpected, we increase the possibility of successfully overcoming anything that might come our way. For Abraham, his time of preparation allowed his men to leave the war victorious because they were able to fight as one cohesive and well-disciplined unit. The valuable time that would have been spent trying to organize his men was instead used in pursuit and defeat of the enemy.

We are told in Scripture that even the animals of God's kingdom know how to prepare:

Proverbs 6:

(6) **Go to the ant, you sluggard; consider its ways and be wise!**

(7) **It has no commander, no overseer or ruler,**

(8) **Yet it stores its provisions in summer and gathers its food at harvest.**

(9) **How long will you lie there, you sluggard? When will you get up from your sleep?**

(10) **A little sleep, a little slumber, a little folding of the hands to rest--**

(11) **And poverty will come on you like a bandit and scarcity like an armed man.** (NIV)

When faced with problems, no matter how gifted you are, preparation will always be necessary.

Consider someone who is called to a life in the medical field. Although they may have tested at the top of their class intellectually and possess a true desire to be a doctor, unless they fulfill the minimum requirements through college, attend medical school, and complete a residence, they will never obtain the title of doctor. The benefit of their preparation, otherwise known as the outcome of the promise, is the designated end in the result or title of doctor. This cannot be accomplished without obtaining the necessary prerequisites - in other words, by being prepared.

The same is true with an athlete who desires to be a world champion. Even though the desire and payoff is to be recognized as the best in the world, this title will not be received without many hours of preparation, sweat from workouts, and physical training. Time must be spent in the study of the technical aspects of the sport to achieve technical proficiency or excellence.

A time of preparation is needed to establish oneself as a contender worthy of the opportunity to participate on the world's stage. When this happens, success is inevitable. Yet success is not found in the end result of the final event, but instead through many hours of preparation that pave the way to receive the ultimate promise.

The Success Formula for any endeavor is this:
Plan before beginning...
Prepare before necessary...
Produce when given the opportunity...
Preparation plus Opportunity will always equal Success.
(Preparation + Opportunity = Success)

For Mediation: Why is it smart to prepare for problems and expect the unexpected in life?

(Matthew 24:44) **"For this reason you also must be ready; for the Son of Man is coming at an hour when you do not think He will.** (NAS95)

(Titus 3:1) **Put them in mind...to be ready to every good work,**
(KJV)

18

DON'T BE FOOLED BY THE PACKAGING OF THE PROMISE

(Genesis 13:10-12) **And Lot lifted up his eyes, and saw that the Jordan valley was well watered everywhere like the garden of the LORD... So Lot chose for himself all the Jordan valley.... Abram dwelt in the land of Canaan, while Lot dwelt among the cities of the valley and moved his tent as far as Sodom.** (RSV)

The greatest deception men suffer is from their own opinions.
Leonardo da Vinci

P romises are often packaged differently from what we might expect. Just as a gift under the Christmas tree is often judged by its wrapping, so we often judge the blessings of God at face value.

In the Genesis 13: 10-12, Abraham and Lot find themselves at a crossroads that will divide them for the rest of their lives. Because Abraham was so blessed, Lot was blessed, as well. Due to the abundance of their blessings in countless possessions, servants, and livestock, they found it difficult to survive in the same land together. Lot and Abraham needed room to stretch out from one another to quell the arguments between their groups of servants.

In an effort to keep the peace, Abraham asked Lot to choose the direction that he would go. After surveying the available territory, Lot chose the land that he believed to be the best choice. It was a land full of water (which was the equivalent to gold in that area), a land that was fertile, and that appeared to allow Lot's possessions to multiply even more. Lot, in evaluating the territory, looked only at the surface and not beyond. He was guilty of the proverbial "judging a book by its cover".

Abraham, who was not only the patriarch but who was also the holder of the promise, was entitled to the land of his choice. It even made sense that because Abraham had more cattle and livestock, he would have received the land that was more fertile with plenty of water. God had told Abraham that he was blessed and had seen fit to bless him with countless cattle, so one would have thought that the land of Sodom was his. But Abraham settled for a land that appeared to be second best.

Since the land looked lush and fertile, Lot was led by a lust that was fed by the physical rather than the spiritual eye. Lot failed to see that it was the presence of God that would bring about a blessing. The presence of God in a desert is always better than a lush and fertile land without God's presence.

In this situation, we find two components at work here:

1. You must never be moved by what is seen on the surface, but rather by what lies beneath. Even though a geologist uses

topographical features, his primary source of research is the charts that depict what lies below the surface.

As an example, consider all of the reservation lands of Oklahoma. In the 1800s, the United States government was searching for a solution in how to deal with the Indian problem. The government decided to take the lands that they had lived on for centuries. These lands provided not only their food but everything that was necessary for their way of life.

The government then decided to send the Indians to reservations, which were thought to be on worthless land in the hills of Oklahoma. In time, these lands proved to be rich with oil, making the poor, impoverished Indians very wealthy. The government believed that the land they had given to the Indians was not valuable and worth very little.

In this circumstance, the worth of the land was not obvious but hidden and what had been intended for bad was eventually turned around for good. God promises us as believers and people of the promise, as he promised Abraham, "I will curse those that curse you" and will turn evil into good.

We find this truth again in Romans:

(Romans 8:28) **And we know that all things work together for good to them that love God, to them who are the called according to his purpose.**

In the story of Joseph, after being sold into slavery by his brothers, he rose to the second highest position in the Egyptian government, second only to the King. When Joseph's brothers came to buy food from the Egyptian government, they bowed before him, and he recounted the story of how his brothers sold him into slavery with bad intent.

Yet again, what his brothers had intended for bad, God intended for good:

(Genesis 50:16) **So they sent a message to Joseph, saying, "Your father gave this command before he died,**

(17) Say to Joseph, Forgive, I pray you, the transgression of your brothers and their sin, because they did evil to you.' And now, we pray you, forgive the transgression of the servants of the God of your father." Joseph wept when they spoke to him.

(18) His brothers also came and fell down before him, and said, "Behold, we are your servants."

(19) **But Joseph said to them, "Fear not, for am I in the place of God?**

(20) **As for you, you meant evil against me; but God meant it for good, to bring it about that many people should be kept alive, as they are today.** (RSV)

2. "Pretty" is inconsequential with the promise. We often look at a car and are only concerned with its external appearance. However, we must check the internal mechanisms, like how the engine runs, if the transmission shifts smoothly and correctly, and if the car doesn't smoke or burn oil, to ensure that it is sound and will run well. Many people will buy a car simply because it is the model and type of car that they want. They will pick a Mercedes for the name alone, forgetting that the purpose of a car is to provide transportation.

God is always more concerned with functionality versus fashion.

God, in his infinite wisdom, may choose to give us a common car, such as a Ford or a Dodge, because it is sound and will provide us with years of service. We may want to purchase our dream car that looks good and has a prestigious name, but God knows that it is not mechanically sound and that it may be on the verge of breaking down.

In the same way, a house inspector realizes that even though a house looks good from the curb, he cannot base his judgment on the exterior alone. He understands that the foundation of the house is most important and inspects it for damages that may be hidden. Lot took the opposite approach by looking only at the outer appearance of the land and was fooled as a result. Sodom, because of its inhabitants, was toxic. We see in the coming chapters of Genesis that it was destroyed because of its sinful nature.

Beware that you don't look with the eyes of flesh instead of the eyes of the spirit when pursuing the promise.

God's Long-Term View

It's no secret that we look at things much differently from God. God plans for the long-term, and we are concerned about the here and now. We will often fail to focus on the future of a situation and instead only focus on our current state. We must learn to look beyond today toward tomorrow, just as God has looked past our current state and focuses on what we will be when His promise is fulfilled.

Remember: Do not place more emphasis on the package than you do on the process.

What God has for you is not based on today's appearance. This is an important truth that we must remember about God's guidance regarding our spouse, home, job, and all opportunities that are placed before us; how will our lives be affected not just today, but years from now? God sees the end from the beginning, He sees the many promises and blessings that He has planned for our future, and He encourages us to look past the external as we pursue the eternal promise.

For Meditation: In what way(s) is God's point of view infinitely superior to ours?

(1 Samuel 16:7) **But the LORD said unto Samuel, Look not on his countenance, or on the height of his stature; because I have refused him: for the LORD seeth not as man seeth; for man looketh on the outward appearance, but the LORD looketh on the heart.**

(1 Corinthians 2:9-14) **However, as it is written: "No eye has seen, no ear has heard, no mind has conceived what God has prepared for those who love him" -- but God has revealed it to us by his Spirit. The Spirit searches all things, even the deep things of God. For who among men knows the thoughts of a man except the man's spirit within him? In the same way no one knows the thoughts of God except the Spirit of God. We have not received the spirit of the world but the Spirit who is from God, that we may understand what God has freely given us. This is what we speak, not in words taught us by human wisdom but in words taught by the Spirit, expressing spiritual truths in spiritual words. The man without the Spirit does not accept the things that come from the Spirit of God, for they are foolishness to him, and he cannot understand them, because they are spiritually discerned.** (NIV)

(1 John 2:27) **As for you, the anointing which you received from Him abides in you, and you have no need for anyone to teach you; but as His anointing teaches you about all things, and**

is true and is not a lie, and just as it has taught you, you abide in Him. (NAS95)

19

PURPOSE

(Genesis 15:7) **He also said to him, "I am the LORD, who brought you out of Ur of the Chaldeans to give you this land to take possession of it."** (NIV)

Not long ago, I needed to attach something with a nail, but I had no hammer. After a search through my tool box, I didn't find a hammer, but found a large wrench that would do in this emergency situation, and I successfully completed my task. Today, I again needed to attach something with a nail, but used a hammer instead of the wrench. Why? Because, although successful with the wrench, the task was awkward and more difficult than necessary. The wrench was intended to turn screws, not to pound nails. Such is the case when we operate outside of our purpose. Although we might be successful with our endeavor, any task done outside of our purpose takes more effort than it naturally should. –B.R.

T hroughout the centuries, men and women of great knowledge and intelligence have wrestled with two primary questions: what is life, and why am I here? In turn, with just a touch of sarcasm, we must ask: after all these years, shouldn't we have some idea?

(1 Corinthians 1:20) **Where is the one who is wise? Where is the scribe? Where is the debater of this age? Has not God made foolish the wisdom of the world?** (NRSV)

Shouldn't there be some template, or some three step program that would transform those in search of their purpose from scared, confused, and timid to bold, certain, and self-assured? Imagine the fortunes to be made, if only such a magical elixir existed.

Did God intend for purpose and fulfillment in life to be so elusive? Out of all of the things He talked about through his Word, one would think that He would have covered the subject in detail and that the answers would be obvious. But then again, could it be that, just as we have confused and distorted "what it is to be a Christian" over the ages, we have also lost sight of what it is to fulfill our purpose and live out our destiny. Have we merely created extraneous questions while in pursuit of our answers--questions that lead to more questions rather than the answer?

(1 Corinthians 1:27) **But God chose what is foolish in the world to shame the wise; God chose what is weak in the world to shame the strong;** (NRSV)

Have we made it much harder than it has to be?

(Genesis 1:27-28) **So God created humankind in his image, in the image of God he created them; male and female he created them. God blessed them, and God said to them, "Be fruitful and multiply, and fill the earth and subdue it; and have dominion over the fish of the sea and over the birds of the air and over every living thing that moves upon the earth."** (NRSV)

Before we proceed any further with the topic of purpose, it is essential that we establish the references within this section that are made regarding Adam, or wording such as his, him, or "man" is not intended to be gender specific. The reference to man in Genesis 1:27 refers to mankind. As the verse states, he made man in his image, male and female.

When God placed mankind on earth he gave fairly simple insight and instructions as to what his purpose, or reason for being was, and what his life was to be about. But notice, before we are told what man is to do, we are told who he is. He is created in the likeness of God. To appreciate the quality of our likeness, we must observe what it means more fully.

First of all, it means that our purpose is linked to our creator. C.S. Lewis said, "God cannot give us a happiness and peace apart from Himself, because it is not there. There is no such thing." If happiness and peace cannot be found apart from God, then that thing that is the source of happiness, purpose, cannot be found apart from God. In other words, rather than seeking our purpose, we should spend more time seeking our purpose giver. If we are part of a divine plan, then we should seek the answers from the divine. To commune with him means to remain in good standing with him, which requires that we live as he commanded, in his likeness.

To be like something, means we are not that thing, but a duplicate, sharing similar qualities, characteristics and traits. Most importantly, we must realize that we are created in the image of a great and powerful God. Although we are not the creators of the universe, we have been duly authorized to act as his representatives. Whatever we commission in his name, as long as it is according to his will, shall be put in effect just as if God said it himself. The reason so many of us are afraid of great life purposes, is because we see ourselves as small and insignificant. It is imperative that we remember that we are powerful, because He is powerful. A police officer of slight stature has the same official authority of an officer of larger size. His authority is not based upon his stature, but rather, by the governmental agency that conferred the power on him. We too have received a confirmation of our power:

(John 14:12-14) **Very truly, I tell you, the one who believes in me will also do the works that I do and, in fact, will do greater works than these, because I am going to the Father. I will do**

whatever you ask in my name, so that the Father may be glorified in the Son. If in my name, you ask me for anything, I will do it. (NRSV)

We have been guaranteed the full support of heaven through the confirmation of God's blessing. Notice an important point found at the beginning of Verse 28 of Genesis 1. After God created man, and just before giving instructions, God, in a similar manner to his initial appearance to Abraham, blesses him. By placing a blessing upon his creation, God releases power upon the recipients, enabling them to succeed at the task that lay before them.

Jesus, the son of God, stated that his purpose in life was to make the lives of believers better, or as He said "life more abundant." In the above verse, he states that he has authorized us to do greater works than he did. Greater than give sight to the blind; greater than making the mute talk and the deaf hear! Yes, with such a great promise, why are we afraid of any task or challenge?

Within the task given to man in the garden of creation lay the keys to the purpose of man and the power for his success. After we are told that man was created in the image of God and blessed by God, he was told to be fruitful, multiply and subdue the earth. Then lastly, toward the completion of the previous instructions, man is told to have dominion over all the other creatures. So what does this mean to the People of Promise thousands of years later?

God tells mankind to be fruitful- to create, produce and bring forth fruit. Then man is to multiply- we are to grow and increase. Lastly man is to subdue and take dominion over the earth- we are to control our lives and all that has been entrusted to our care rather than let it control us. Let's examine each of these concepts in greater detail.

Although most would interpret fruitful more strictly, the strict interpretation would mean mankind's only purpose is to reproduce like rabbits, but that can't be our purpose in life. *If we separate the commands and look at them as two distinct commands: be fruitful, then multiply, we are able to see more clearly what God intended.*

A vine or branch is termed "fruitful" when it yields that which it was designed to bear, especially when it does so in abundance; or is termed barren or worthless when it does not produce as intended. This is the case with all humans. Each person is designed to bring some fruit into the world. And just as the type of fruits vary from plant to plant, and tree to tree, so will our fruits vary from person to person.

Because we are designed to be fruitful, we are at our best, *we feel our best*, when we are producing, bringing forth fruit from our toil in this world, regardless of what that toil might be. At the end of a productive day, how do you feel? If you have done good work, if you left a piece of yourself there in the work, don't you feel fruitful; productive or successful, even fulfilled? Of course, because humans were designed with a need to produce, and once they have produced, they want to produce more and more and more…. Whether it be from sowing and reaping seed from the earth, creating some artistic masterpiece with paint and canvas, repairing planes, trains and automobile, or seeing to it that their child is provided for in the best way possible, we all find a great sense of fulfillment in knowing that we have contributed something positive in this world.

Ironically, this is exactly the opposite of what the world seems designed for. So often people are preoccupied with the pursuit of pleasures and entertainment that they are distracted from any kind of fruitful work. Even though most dream and hope for a life of ease and relaxation; eventually that would become old with no opportunity to produce and appreciate our fruit. This is a fact that can be proven by the most productive in our society; they realized that retirement from one career simply meant the beginning of some new project. They understood that to grow in purpose- to produce something positive in this earth is necessary for mankind's ultimate satisfaction. For to be fruitful is to be fulfilled, and to stop doing, is to start dying!!

The final part of the command shows us what resources we have at our disposal to be fruitful. Imagine, you want to build something, but with what materials? God told Adam and Eve that the entire earth, all plants, all animals, everything in the earth would be subject, or available to them to ensure their success. Whatever they had need of, was theirs to be used as they saw fit because they were given dominion! Dominion means to have supreme authority. In other words, God duly authorized them to make and enact plans, utilizing the resources as they decided, to succeed at the job he had assigned them. God too, has given you dominion over this world to utilize his unlimited resources to be successful.

However, that last part of the command also holds a warning for us. Just as Adam and Eve were placed in the garden as caretakers, so are we placed in the world. And, just as Adam and Eve forgot that although they were given dominion in the earth and in the heavens, they were still subject to the one that possessed ultimate dominion, as are we. We must never lose sight of the responsibility to take care of the resources God gave us. Like a parent leaving His children under the care of a sitter, God expects us to take good care of the Earth and animals. So, while we want to be productive in our purposeful life, we mustn't help destroy the earth in the name of fruitfulness.

Just as we must be good stewards of the natural resources God has provided, so must we be careful stewards of the opportunities he places in our path. We all know of Adams "original sin in the garden"- but he committed a second sin, which I believe was just as condemning in the garden that day. Adam and Eve squandered their opportunity to live the life God purposed them to live.

Adam and Eve were placed in the Garden of Eden and purposed with its' management and oversight; they were given unlimited resources to use as they deemed necessary. And yet, as you remember, they failed miserably. Their purpose had been established and resources provided. What could possibly go wrong? What goes wrong today? To answer this final question we must events that transpired after man's creation:

Genesis 3

1 Now the serpent was more subtle than any other wild creature that the LORD God had made. He said to the woman, "Did God say, 'You shall not eat of any tree of the garden'?"

2 And the woman said to the serpent, "We may eat of the fruit of the trees of the garden;

3 but God said, 'You shall not eat of the fruit of the tree which is in the midst of the garden, neither shall you touch it, lest you die.'"

4 But the serpent said to the woman, "You will not die.

5 For God knows that when you eat of it your eyes will be opened, and you will be like God, knowing good and evil."

6 So when the woman saw that the tree was good for food, and that it was a delight to the eyes, and that the tree was

to be desired to make one wise, she took of its fruit and ate; and she also gave some to her husband, and he ate.

7 Then the eyes of both were opened, and they knew that they were naked; and they sewed fig leaves together and made themselves aprons.

8 And they heard the sound of the LORD God walking in the garden in the cool of the day, and the man and his wife hid themselves from the presence of the LORD God among the trees of the garden.

9 But the LORD God called to the man, and said to him, "Where are you?"

10 And he said, "I heard the sound of thee in the garden, and I was afraid, because I was naked; and I hid myself." (RSV)

Once more we look at Jesus' stated purpose on earth in comparison to that of the enemy:

(John 10:10) **The thief comes only to steal and kill and destroy; I have come that they may have life, and have it to the full.** (NIV)

Jesus states he has come so that each person might experience life to the "full." In other words, life would be so good, you couldn't contain any more. On the other hand, the enemy seeks to diminish our time on earth by stealing, killing and destroying. Our enemy desires that we experience lesser amounts than possible. And just as Jesus desires for our lives to be full, the devil hopes that our container of life would be empty, one single drop of fulfillment would be a drop too much.

How did the enemy destroy those lives of purpose and promise? What techniques did he use ages ago in the garden and still in our lives today? First of all, the enemy attempts to bring confusion regarding your purpose and instruction. He poses the question to Eve in Verse 1, "Did God say?" Notice, Eve wasn't told that God hadn't spoken, just made to doubt *what* he said. The enemy's primary tool is to make you unsure of what you are to do and how you are to do it. Every person has been given the ability to hear the Divine Voice of guidance and wisdom in your life. The ability to hear increases over time, so don't become discouraged in the beginning. Here's an example that just about everyone reading this book will relate to. When I was a boy growing up, and I did something wrong in a crowd, especially in church, my Mother had a way of clearing her throat to get my attention. Now of course, this was the same method all the other mothers in our church used as well. Interestingly, it didn't take long to distinguish my mother's "ugh...em" from that of the other mothers. As I matured it even got to the point that her 'throat clear' became an unspoken language, alerting me to stop what I was doing immediately. Each of us possess the ability to hear and interpret God's directions for our life, we simply have to distinguish His voice from the enemy and other distractions of life. Once you know it, you have to listen intently in the beginning until it becomes second nature.

Secondly, the enemy caused Eve to question God's Word in verses three and four, assuring her that what God vowed would happen, would not. We have discussed the validity and authority of God's Word previously in chapter 3, The Particulars of the Promise. Perhaps this would be a good time to re-confirm in your mind that what God says, God does.

The enemy's last attempt was his most subtle, yet most effective tool; he appealed to Eve's ego. Ego is easily manipulated; even the most secure persons can be made to doubt themselves, and those with low self-esteem made foolish with pride. In the course of one sentence, the enemy was able to make Eve question her God-given position and instill in her an ego driven desire to be God's equal.

(Genesis 3:5) **For God knows that when you eat of it your eyes will be opened, and <u>you will be like</u> God, knowing good and evil."** (NRSV)

Sadly, Adam and Eve were manipulated into sin because they forgot for a split second who they were created to be. They were already like God, formed in his very image, given all necessary power and authority to rule; to rule all over all the earth, even to rule over the enemy that sought to betray them.

Our enemy the snake continues to slither around the gardens of our lives hoping to outwit the people of the promise, craftily condemning each person to a life that is less than what God hoped by stealing, killing and destroying. The enemy steals our purpose, our foundation for a fulfilling life. He kills our hope, the source of our passion. A life without hope is no life at all, it is merely an existence anchored in despair! With no purpose to fulfill and no passion to energize us, life becomes a curse rather than a blessing; it becomes a test of survival, rather than a glorious and victorious procession through life.

Remember, God wants you to succeed at being you! He picked you for your purpose, specifically designed you for your destiny, provided for every need you might have in the pursuit of your promises!!

For Meditation: How do many people feel about their purpose? How are they right, and how could you help them?

(Isaiah 14:27) **For the LORD of hosts has purposed, And who will annul it? His hand is stretched out, And who will turn it back?"** (NKJV)

(2 Timothy 1:9) **Who hath saved us, and called us with an holy calling, not according to our works, but according to his own purpose and grace, which was given us in Christ Jesus before the world began,**

(Romans 8:28) **And we know that all things work together for good to those who love God, to those who are the called according to His purpose.** (NKJV)

(Ephesians 1:11-12) **In him we were also chosen, having been predestined according to the plan of him who works out everything in conformity with the purpose of his will, in order that we, who were the first to hope in Christ, might be for the praise of his glory.** (NIV)

20

THE PROMISE IS PROPELLED BY PASSION

(Romans 4:19) **He did not weaken in faith when he considered his own body, which was as good as dead because he was about a hundred years old...** (RSV)

Passion is the element in which we live; without it, we hardly vegetate. – Lord Byron

Our passions are the winds that propel our vessel. Our reason is the pilot that steers her. Without winds the vessel would not move and without a pilot she would be lost. – Proverbs

There is no greatness without a passion to be great...
— Anthony Robbins

Passion is the difference between mediocrity and SUPERIORITY.

Passion is the power that propels you to purpose.

Passion is the catalyst of creativity.

Passion is an anchor in turbulent times.

Passion overcomes ALL obstacles.

No great thing can be accomplished without passion.

- B. R.

P assion in its' simplest form is nothing more than energy. It is never a mandatory component to any action; numerous deeds, many worthy of notoriety, are completed daily without it. However, it is doubtful that any great deed, one that changes the course of history, has ever been completed without passion. Passion can be constructive or destructive, focused or uncontrolled. But when controlled and used positively, it will yield results that no amount of proficiency or skill can produce alone.

Perhaps you have heard the term "crime of passion" used during a courtroom proceeding to describe the overwhelming rush of emotional energy experienced by a defendant before committing a crime. Or perhaps, a "work of passion", used to describe the amazing accomplishment of some artist or performer who reached beyond normal human expectation. No matter the case, it was the passion, the fire that burned within, that produced the superior results.

At some time in your life, you have undoubtedly been assisted by a store clerk that made you feel as if you were impeding their space and time by merely asking for assistance. Or perhaps you have witnessed those individuals moving through the normal duties of life who barely seem to have enough energy to take the next step, much less make it to their destination. These are examples of lives that are void of passion, seen daily anywhere you look: at your place of employment, on the streets of our neighborhoods, within our places of worship and even our homes. To walk among those who are devoid of passion, is very much like living among, if not being a member of "the walking dead."

Passion, a deep stirring or ungovernable emotion, can make the most mundane of tasks seem enjoyable, and what would normally be viewed as painful, pleasurable. Passion stirs your innermost being, releasing something inside you that can propel you to levels of creativity and performance that allow you to operate at a far superior level than that of colleagues or other participants.

There are countless testimonies of those who speak of being possessed by something from within that resulted in some work that transcended commonly accepted barriers. It has been said, "My mind was taken out of the equation and seemed to be on auto-pilot... the idea came from someplace other than myself... I was truly inspired." By understanding the meaning of "inspired," we are able to understand the source of such accomplishment. The term inspired means to be in spirit, or stated differently, not controlled by self. When we operate in spirit, our creative juices flow, the embers of passion are stoked, and superior outcomes are guaranteed. We are no longer operating on an earthly plane, where we are anchored by human conditions and limited thinking, but we are lifted to a place where mental and creative abilities are merged and allowed to function without regard to what we would normally hold to be fact.

Inspiration is not just the source of creative passion it is also the source of enduring passion. When you are inspired, or in spirit, not only are the limits of thought and creativity broken, but so are your normal barriers of mental and physical discomfort. When inspired, your pain threshold is raised, and obstacles that once seemed overwhelming are reduced to mere bumps in the road. Passion will truly propel you through the process to your promise.

So, how is that one loses passion? Although some lose their passion because of some major tragedy of life, most lose it gradually; little by little... in small quantities over periods of time. Because the losses are small and scattered over time, the ever-growing void goes un-noticed, until, one awakes one day to realize that life has become a burden rather than a blessing. A new day is despised rather than anticipated and joy jumped ship a long time ago. Hope and happiness have been depleted and just surviving has become difficult within itself. Although our natural reaction is to lament for the poor broken souls that have fallen to such levels, we fail to realize that you and I, if we have not arrived at that place already, are sure to meander down that path as well, if we are not ever conscious of our daily choices and actions.

So, how can you be assured of passion throughout life? First, you must realize that IF you don't live life, it will live you! In the opening pages of the Bible, we find the story of Adam at his swearing in ceremony as keeper of the garden. As the "caretakers," he and Eve were authorized by God, according to Genesis 2:15 NIV, to "work it and take care of it." In that same spirit God has authorized us to work what we have been given and to take care of it. For the most part, we are only partly affected by chance, but totally subject to choice. Since choice is the chief determinant in each person's life, you must make wise and well-informed choices that will advance you toward your promise, rather than allowing the winds of chance to direct you where it may. Each day, choose to use what you have been given charge of wisely; leave nothing under your control to chance. Choose to treat others as you desire to be treated, choose to make the most of each opportunity, choose to be wise, choose to be healthy, choose to be happy... choose to create a life where passion can abound.

Secondly, relationships with the wrong people will suppress passion. On the path to promise, it will be necessary to part company with certain people in our lives. Many people believe that because a person is in their life today, they will be there tomorrow. They waste precious energy and time attempting to keep dying relationships alive. The truth is, in life we all travel different roads, and some roads diverge great distances, distances too great to continue the relationship. Many, who began the process of the Promise with you, are not intended to end the process with you.

In the first verses of Genesis chapter 12, when God gives Abraham the command to leave Haran, God makes no mention of his nephew Lot. However, not only does Lot accompany Abraham, he also becomes wealthy because of the blessing that rests on Abraham. Unfortunately, by Chapter 13, their wealth has become a matter of contention between the two, so much so that their servants have begun to argue with each other. Although the Bible does not say that Abraham and Lot encountered difficulties between them, it seems very likely that their relationship was strained as well. In an effort to dispel the hostility between them, Abraham asks Lot to choose which direction he and his household will go, and he in turn will go the opposite direction. Abraham had wandered the countryside for years with his nephew in tow, searching for the Promised Land to no avail, but, as soon as they have parted ways, God reveals to Abraham the land of his inheritance. For whatever reason, Abraham was unable to receive the promise of God, until he and Lot were separated. There are some relationships in our life that will suspend our promises, and thereby, must be ended. Contentious relationships will always cause internal strife; if those negative relationships are allowed to continue, the resulting confusion will stifle our spirits and cause passion to go missing.

The most prevalent cause for loss of passion is loss of true self. The world, with all of its technology and information, has become increasingly difficult to navigate and to establish one's sense of self. The long asked question, "Who am I?" has become increasingly difficult to answer rather than simpler. Today, the vast majority of people have no idea who they are, and unfortunately, marketers know this. Sadly, marketers also know an empty sponge will absorb anything. If exposed to their marketing messages repeatedly, these multitudes comprised of adults as well as youth, will accept the identity offered by these marketers, rather than seek their own.

Today, those who are insightful enough to seek their own identity, often go to great lengths to make personal statements of individuality. This leads to the questions, "What is true individualism?" Is having multicolored hair (really, is hair supposed to be every color of the rainbow?), or wearing clothes 4 sizes too big, true individualism, or, some misguided attempt? Because one person does something different, I desire to do the same thing to make a statement....Is that true individualism? True individualism flows from the inside out, never from the outside in. In other words, true individualism will never see something outside itself and seek to mimic or surpass it. But rather, it will flow from within to the outside world, with no desire to be spoken of or noticed, but its only necessary acknowledgment is being.

I witnessed a young woman being interviewed on TV not long ago, whose body was covered in tattoos. "Why so many?" she was asked by the reporter. Her reply, "I want my body to make a statement about my individuality...I don't know if I will ever have enough." While this is truly not an indictment of those with tattoos, it does raise some important questions that get to the heart of the matter: Why does she feel the need to make a statement? Why is she not the statement? Why is the individuality of her inner beauty not enough, or her warm smile or warm personality? Why do so many people feel who they naturally are; their qualities, traits, strengths, weaknesses and all, are not enough to distinguish them from others? Nothing outside can make any greater distinction between you and another person as much as anything inside of you. Perhaps this would be a great time to review Chapter 6: Promised People Appear Peculiar! In a nutshell: Be you... DO YOU... because you are the only person you can do well!!

Passion requires authenticity of self and purpose to flourish. The minute you act in a way that does not resonate with your core beliefs and qualities - who you really are - you can be sure that passion will vanish.

"To thine own self be true" - Shakespeare

To be authentic in self and purpose requires that you trust the voice within. The authentic voice springs from your soul, it is the voice of true self. Time and distance has estranged many of us from our inner voice. Many have ignored the voice of true self so long that they have forgotten the sweet and soothing sound and its ability to gently lead you that place of contentment. Rest assured the voice still speaks....just trust and keep listening. To hear and respond to your inner voice is to find a wellspring of passion!

Finally, the most surprising reason for the death of passion is that we can actually lose contact with and forget about the things that ignite our passions. We become so preoccupied with the concerns of life, that we lose touch with the things that bring true joy into our life. Some years ago, I lost touch with my most beloved passion, music. For most of my life, even dating back to elementary school, music of all kinds filled my life. Music was an extension of who I was at my core. For most of my life, dating back to my sophomore year of high school, I worked as an on-air personality (deejay) for numerous different radio stations during the day, all day; I dee-jayed for clubs and parties half the night. But still, as soon as I got home, the stereo was turned on immediately. Many nights I would stay up well into the morning hours, listening to different pieces, searching for new phrases and riffs that might have gone unnoticed the prior 100 times I had listened to the song. Then, unconsciously, I let my one true love, slip away. After marrying and moving into a new home, things were so hectic and my daily routine so different, that I never got around to hooking up my beloved stereo. From one set of preoccupations to another, I never found the time to get my music up and going, although, in all of my previous moves, the stereo was the first thing assembled and the last thing to be packed. Somehow or another, what was supposed to be a delay of a few days turned into many years. Even more amazingly, I never realized what I had done, or actually hadn't done. Yes, in the early days and months of our separation, I knew something was missing. I just never had actually taken the time to stop and think about what was absent from my life. Then, one night several years later, totally by accident, while my family was away, in a solitary moment when I found myself alone with my thoughts, a familiar melody came to mind. In a spontaneous instance, the urge to hear this song couldn't be contained and I assembled my long lost and forgotten friend. After only a few bars of the song, I was overcome by a distant, yet not forgotten feeling of euphoria. My soul was stirred in its' deepest reaches; places within me felt touched like the first warm day of spring after a long cold winter. Those places that had lain barren were suddenly alive again. I will never forget the feeling I encountered that night, the feeling of a dead soul being resurrected. Now, that music has found its way back into my life, I don't intend to forget about the joy that it brings me. And, except for brief interventions due to life's demands, it will never remain absent for any extended period of time ever again.

It is your responsibility to seek out the things that bring joy and passion to your life. Once found, it is your responsibility to hold on to that source of joy and passion. Hold on, as if your life depends on it, because it does! Without passion, your Purpose becomes unimportant. And without passion, Power is impossible.

For Meditation: What is meant by "passion" in this chapter? Why is this important?

(Romans 12:11) **Never be lacking in zeal, but keep your spiritual fervor, serving the Lord.** (NIV)

(Colossians 3:17 & 23) **And whatever you do, in word or deed, do everything in the name of the Lord Jesus, giving thanks to God the Father through him... Whatever your task, put yourselves into it, as done for the Lord and not for your masters** (NRSV)

21

YOUR GREATEST POWER LIES WITHIN YOUR PROMISE

(Genesis 23:6) **"Hear us, my lord, you are a mighty prince among us..."** (NASB)

(Genesis 20:7) **"Now therefore, restore the man's wife, for he is a prophet, and he will pray for you, and you will live. But if you do not restore her, know that you shall surely die, you and all who are yours."** (MKJV)

POWER- Pow-er\ˈpau̇(-ə)r\
1. legal or official authority, capacity, or right
2. ability to act or produce an effect
3. capacity for being acted upon or undergoing an effect
4. possession of control, authority, or influence over others

T he Apostle Paul, in the early lines of his second letter to Timothy, takes a moment to remind Timothy of the God-given purpose and power instilled in him to complete his appointed task:

(2Ti 1:6) **For this reason I remind you to rekindle the gift of God that is within you through the laying on of my hands;**

(2Ti 1:7) **for God did not give us a spirit of cowardice, but rather a spirit of power and of love and of self-discipline.** (NRSV)

Paul realized that Timothy, regardless of the qualities and abilities he had been given, would benefit from a supportive reminder of his position in God. The power, or *dunamis* as it is written in the Greek text, refers to the ability and strength, or special ability bestowed upon Timothy that would ensure success in all endeavors. Today, we like Timothy, need to be reminded of the power that lies within.

That same power is not merely implied, but expressed through the commands of God; where he guides he provides. There is no place that He will send you, and no task that He will assign you, that you are not prepared to succeed. It is true, many times we begin things that are beyond our skill set and ability. However, because God has appointed you to that task, he has also appointed the necessary skills and/or means for the appointed time to ensure that you have what you need when you need it.

Dictionaries define power many different ways, but each is synonymous with influence. Power's most simple definition is the ability to effect change, through influence or pressure. Conversely, power can be displayed through the ability to withstand the effects of applied pressure or influence. The ability to effect change in and on the lives of those he came in contact with; and the ability to keep external pressure from denying his life promises, demonstrate the power bestowed upon Abraham.

Each person of promise has received the same type of power that God placed upon the life of Abraham. The power bestowed upon us by God is best described as having similar characteristics to steel. Steel is one of the strongest substances known to man. But to the average eye steel is un-assuming; it is lifeless and non-threatening -- until it is utilized to accomplish an end. In the hands of a master craftsman, it can be transformed into a great work of art; wielded by an attacker on a dark street, even a small length of it can be deadly. Steel though rigid and strong, when tempered, is moldable and flexible and suitable for use in accomplishing many great tasks. It is used to build the tallest buildings, to provide shelter and appease our eyes. It is used to manufacture planes, trains and automobiles, to transport us and make our lives easier. The power of our promises is exactly the same. When utilized to an end, there is nothing like it. Although intangible and undetected by the human eye, its' effects are seen and realized for years after.

The power promised to you by God assures your success. Because we are the spiritual seed of Abraham, we possess this power as well. However, just like a pauper who had been willed a fortune by a wealthy relative that he has never met, so are the people of the promise, rightful heirs and legal owners, yet unaware and poverty stricken.

As in the case with passion, there are countless numbers of people upon the face of the earth today, who are unaware of the Power that is inherent with the Promise.

Most people live powerless lives because they are operating outside of purpose, and thereby outside of their promise. To better explain the process and the significance of power, examine the following scenario, all though oversimplified, it should provide greater clarity:

Imagine one of God's chosen people, is ordained to dig a great lake in a geographical area that desperately needs water. This lake will allow water to be gathered, so that people as well as wildlife will have an ample water supply. In this case, the promises of God would prepare his chosen person by first placing within him or her, an interest in some related subject, such as geology, the environment, the strategic use of natural resources or perhaps heavy construction. This desire might be further fuelled by a desire to help those in need, possibly, the populations of undeveloped areas or nations.

The promise would then direct this person to the proper place or proper person(s) to gain knowledge of this community that suffers from the lack of water. This information might be gained through established relationships or possibly through a serendipitous meeting with a total stranger. For the person of promise, the natural love of the subject and the desire to serve form purpose and passion. The encounter and the acknowledged need create an opportunity for purpose to move into action. Now, once true purpose is acted upon, the individual will receive the "power" through the purposes of God to effect the necessary change through any required knowledge, skill, or tool to complete the task. In this situation, power could be represented by the equipment necessary for digging, such as a tractor or backhoe.

This encounter, the natural love of the subject, the desire to serve and a perceived need come together allowing purpose and passion to meet opportunity. Anytime purpose and passion meet at the crossroads of opportunity, power and ultimately success are sure to follow.

To understand our power, let's look at how the Power of the Promise manifest in Abraham's life, according to the definitions of power at the start of the chapter.

1. The possession of legal or official authority, capacity, or right. From the very beginning of Abraham's journey in Genesis 12, God establishes that everything Abraham is to do will be done in his authority. In that initial exchange God states "I Will" six separate times, establishing his authority in the earth, and Abraham's official rights as the bearer of the promise.

I will show you the land (v.1)
I will make you a great nation (v.2)
I will bless you (v.2)
I will make your name great (v.2)
I will bless those who bless you (v.3)
I will curse those that curse you (v. 3)

Each person of promise bears the rights that are inherent to their promise through a sovereign God. Because God has ordained it, you have been authorized to receive what he has promised, just as simple as that.

To understand this more fully, consider America's monetary system. Anyone who possesses currency, for this example a $20 bill, has the right to receive goods or services worth $20 in exchange for the bill of currency. The value of the bill is determined and guaranteed by the issuer. In the case of money, the United States government, not the person in possession of the money sets the value. Such is the case with our promises. We have been issued currency, the promises of God. We are entitled to the exact value of our promise, guaranteed by God, the issuer. Regardless, of what anyone does or says, we are entitled to receive the full value promised as long as we are in possession of that currency. This is the great news of the promise – as long as you hold on to the promises of God, they can never be rejected, denied or discounted. Just as our currency assures us that when the currency is presented it will be accepted as legal tender (payment) in exchange for what is desired, such are the promises that God gave us. Just as we boldly present that earthly currency at retailers and merchants far and wide, we should present God's promises of prosperity and fulfillment to life, with no fear of negative response . After all, just as it is written plainly on the back of that earthly currency, so should that bold declaration be permanently stamped on our hearts and minds- "In God We Trust."

2. The ability to act or produce an effect. Also stated in the beginning verses of Genesis 12 is the effect that Abraham, through his promise, will have upon his descendants and those that he encounters in life (see the verses in #1). The Promise would produce an effect in the lives of everyone who came in contact with it. To those who recognized it and regarded it favorably (I will bless them that bless you) the Power would produce positive effects. But, to those who disregarded and despised the Promise or its' bearer (I will curse them that curse you), the power would be equally potent, but to a negative end.

As an example, Abraham's nephew Lot, was never mentioned as a direct beneficiary to the Promise that was given Abraham, but it is evident that he profited greatly, simply from being in the presence of Abraham.

Now Abram was very rich in livestock, in silver, and in gold...

Now Lot, who went with Abram, also had flocks and herds and tents, so that the land could not support both of them living together; for their possessions were so great that they could not live together... Genesis 13:2, 5-6 (NRSV)

As long as Lot was mindful that the promise given to Abraham was the source of their blessings, everything was held in check and the blessings flowed from God through Abraham and on to Lot. Notice that as long as Lot respected the anointing or Promise placed upon Abraham, he was blessed, but the moment he took it for granted, he started down the path to destruction.

(Genesis 13:8-12) **Then Abram said to Lot, "Let there be no strife between you and me, and between your herders and my herders; for we are kindred. Is not the whole land before you? Separate yourself from me. If you take the left hand, then I will go to the right; or if you take the right hand, then I will go to the left." Lot looked about him, and saw that the plain of the Jordan was well watered everywhere like the garden of the LORD, like the land of Egypt, in the direction of Zoar; this was before the LORD had destroyed Sodom and Gomorrah. So Lot chose for himself all the plain of the Jordan, and Lot journeyed eastward; thus they separated from each other. Abram settled in the land of Canaan, while Lot settled among the cities of the Plain and moved his tent as far as Sodom.** (NRSV)

In this moment of poor judgement Lot forgot how he accumulated all that he had. He forgot it wasn't his wisdom or keen business acumen; it wasn't even his promise. Lot forgot the source of the blessings; he forgot he was blessed because Abraham was blessed. He forgot that the blessings came from the Promise and the power of the promise was not under his control:

(Deuteronomy 8:18) **But remember the LORD your God, for it is he who gives you power to get wealth, so that he may confirm his covenant that he swore to your ancestors, as he is doing today.** (NRSV)

Just as Abraham was a conduit, through which the blessings were to flow, so are we, as bearers of the promise. As we fulfill the mandate on our lives, those that meet us, for even the briefest of moments, will be blessed because of the overflowing blessing and power that emanates from within us.

3. The capacity for being acted upon or undergoing an effect. This might be better explained if viewed as the capacity to withstand, or not be affected by outside influences. As an example, the quality that makes steel so durable is its' ability to withstand applied pressure in varying forms. Steel is capable of bearing heavy

loads as well as withstand high temperatures. Most common combustibles will combust or change form at temperatures of 400 degrees F or below. But, steel has a much higher threshold, responding to temperature near 1800 degrees F .

When heat and pressure is applied in our lives in the form of adversity or trials, humans have a tendency to buckle under that pressure. But, when operating in the Power of our Promise, we too are able to withstand external pressures that would cause us to collapse in normal situations.

During the travels of Abraham, except for a few cases of dishonesty, Abraham remained true to his promise and call. Even though he was born in a geographic area that worshipped many gods, Abraham was able to hear from and obey the one true God. Despite traveling through many unknown alien lands, he was able to keep sight of his unique anointing, even though there was no one else that shared or understood the ordeals that he alone faced. He walked a solitary road, alone.

The ability to remain unaffected by those he encountered should never be marginalized. Because humans are social beings and the need for acceptance is one of our basic needs, we often assimilate what we come in contact with. Although we might begin marching to the beat of a different drum, just like an "out of step" member of a marching band will try to "correct," we intuitively begin adjusting our steps to be like those around us. When allowed to operate fully within you, the Power of your Promise will draw others to you and cause them to desire what you have. Just like each person has a distinct DNA signature, so is the power signature of each person's promise. It is original and exclusive to that one person and promise.

4. The possession of control, authority, or influence over others. Throughout the Bible those called to do the work of God have wielded unusual power over others. This power often resulted in alliances between God's people and their historical enemies. Those possessing this special power of the Lord have been called many things including: anointed of the Lord, blessed of the Lord, and highly favored of the Lord. Regardless of what they were called, the true emphasis should rest on "of the Lord," because God is the source of this mind changing, attitude altering and friendship-forging power that works on the behalf of those of Promise.

Abraham, because of his "blessed" status was often referred to as a prince, or person of royal birthright. During ancient times, royalty reigned supreme; their every command was carried out without hesitation or question. If at any time those commands were ignored, the military force of that nation was under the absolute control of the king or queen to enact their wish. To the nations that encountered Abraham, his status with the "armies" of heaven was recognized and feared. Those who would have been natural enemies offered their support to Abraham in all of his endeavors rather than risk the wrath of God.

Twice Abraham convinced his wife Sarah to lie and say that she was his sister and not his wife because he feared that the kings of foreign lands would desire her for her beauty and kill him to claim her as their wife. In both cases God kept the kings from consummating the marriage, keeping Sarah's honor intact. In chapter 13, to keep the Pharoah of Egypt from violating his divine plan, God sent "great plagues" to afflict Pharoah's house until he realized that taking Abraham's wife was a mistake. In Genesis chapter 20, King Abimelech also desired Abraham's wife, but God intervened. As you read the following account, notice how God intervenes on Abraham's behalf:

(Genesis 20:2-8) **Abraham said of his wife Sarah, "She is my sister." And King Abimelech of Gerar sent and took Sarah. But God came to Abimelech in a dream by night, and said to him, "You are about to die because of the woman whom you have taken; for she is a married woman." Now Abimelech had not approached her; so he said, "Lord, will you destroy an innocent people? Did he not himself say to me, 'She is my sister'? And she herself said, 'He is my brother.' I did this in the integrity of my heart and the innocence of my hands." Then God said to him in the dream, "Yes, I know that you did this in the integrity of your heart; furthermore it was I who kept you from sinning against me. Therefore I did not let you touch her. Now then, return the man's wife; for he is a prophet, and he will pray for you and you shall live. But if you do not restore her, know that you shall surely die, you and all that are yours." So Abimelech rose early in the morning, and called all his servants and told them all these things; and the men were very much afraid.** (NRSV)

God makes it clear to King Abimelech that he acted on the behalf of Abraham; not Abraham himself. Even though Abimelech was an earthly king, even he was subject to the Divine King. In both cases Abraham entered the countries of foreign kings afraid of their status as royalty, not realizing that the King who anointed and authorized him to go forth, wielded the ultimate power to influence and control any opposition he might encounter. In both cases, God's power not only caused kings to yield to the Promise bearer, but just as God promised in Genesis 12:3, they must bless Abraham or risk being cursed. In the end, both kings in an earnest desire to escape the wrath of God sent Abraham away with livestock, servants and other material possessions so that Abraham left their country with much greater wealth than he arrived with.

In a final effort to appease Abraham, King Abimilech actually allows Abraham to choose the place in his kingdom where he would like to live, saying to Abraham, "My land is before you; live wherever you like."

This was the power God promised Abraham--and the power he has promised you. This God-given power will pave the way to your promise. This power will change the mind of those that challenge you, it will make your antagonist agreeable. It will turn adversaries into allies and make enemies empathetic to your cause. In other words, it will make your way successful.

To fully understand the support that God has pledged to each person of Promise, consider God's promise to his servant Joshua. Joshua, Moses' successor, had the final responsibility of leading God's chosen people into the land that God had promised their forefather Abraham more than 600 years before. On the dawn of Abraham's descendants entry into the Promised Land, God reassures Joshua that no matter what he encountered in possessing the Promised Land, the power that went with the people of Promise was greater than any difficulty that lay ahead:

"... Now proceed to cross the Jordan, you and all this people, into the land that I am giving to them, to the Israelites. Every place that the sole of your foot will tread upon I have given to you, as I promised to Moses. From the wilderness and the Lebanon as far as the great river, the river Euphrates, all the land of the Hittites, to the Great Sea in the west shall be your territory. No one shall be able to stand against you all the days of

your life. **As I was with Moses, so I will be with you; I will not fail you or forsake you. Be strong and courageous; for you shall put this people in possession of the land that I swore to their ancestors to give them. Only be strong and very courageous, being careful to act in accordance with all the law that my servant Moses commanded you; do not turn from it to the right hand or to the left, so that you may be successful wherever you go. This book of the law shall not depart out of your mouth; you shall meditate on it day and night, so that you may be careful to act in accordance with all that is written in it. For then you shall make your way prosperous, and then you shall be successful. I hereby command you: Be strong and courageous; do not be frightened or dismayed, for the LORD your God is with you wherever you go."** (Joshua 1:2-9) (NRSV)

For Meditation: What power do you feel you have? How can you use your power for good?

(Ephesians 6:10) **Finally, my brethren, be strong in the Lord and in the power of His might.** (NKJV)

(Deuteronomy 20:4) **for it is the LORD your God who goes with you, to fight for you against your enemies, to give you victory."** (NRSV)

(Proverbs 16:7) **When a man's ways please the LORD, he makes even his enemies to be at peace with him.** (RSV)

22

PROSPERITY IS A BY-PRODUCT OF THE PROMISE

(Genesis 24:1) **Now Abraham was old, advanced in age; and the LORD had blessed Abraham in every way.** (NASB)

(Genesis 24:35) **"And the LORD has greatly blessed my master (Abraham), so that he has become rich; and He has given him flocks and herds, and silver and gold, and servants and maids, and camels and donkeys.** (NASB)

N ot long ago, a close Christian friend of mine asked a question that brought us to one of the few disagreements of our friendship that dates back to grade school. "Do you believe that God desires for everyone to be rich?" he asked, with a cunning tone that hinted he expected a disagreement to follow. My answer of "Yes, I do," was met with an immediate response of, "Well, I don't," complete with a 10 minute laundry list of why he felt God did not intend for His people to expect wealth in their life. I found it interesting at the very least, that we, great friends and both believers, had such a divergent view of the faith we shared.

It wasn't until a few days later, that a mutual friend shed some light on that conversation. "Byron," he said, "The problem is, you lost each other with the word 'rich'. Perhaps he meant rich in money, and you meant rich in life. With many people you have to establish what prosperity or rich truly means... perhaps 'prosperous' would have been the proper term." This was a true "A-ha" moment for me, as I realized that many people will never experience the "rich" life God intended simply because they don't understand prosperity from the perspective of God's kingdom.

True prosperity is so much more than money. However, before I go any further, I need to stress that although prosperity is much more than money, it certainly includes money. After all, Solomon, regarded by many as the wisest and richest man in the history of the world stated:

(Ecclesiastes 10:19) **A feast is made for laughter, and wine makes life merry, but money is the answer for everything.** (NIV)

This wise writer was not advising his readers to value money more than anything else, but rather, he desired that each person understand that money is a necessity of life that must be respected and valued in the proper manner. More detailed readings of the books of Proverbs and Ecclesiastes reveals that Solomon understood that money or material possessions should never be the desired end to attaining happiness. Rather, it was a necessary means.

Most believers will never experience true prosperity in their life because they have been made to believe that money is sinful. Believers and non-believers alike have falsely subscribed to the assumption that salvation must be coupled with starvation, and to have wealth is a sin. Secondly, because wealth is seen as a sin, we have developed negative feelings toward wealth; we subconsciously avoid wealth rather than expect it in our life. But why is that? Why do we believe that faith and finances are like oil and water? Why do so many believe that riches and righteousness must be mutually exclusive? Why is wealth associated with a sinful nature and poverty synonymous with sainthood?

Upon closer observation, it all makes sense. After all, who didn't grow up hearing 1 Timothy 6:10 misquoted for most of their formative years? Time and again we heard "Money is the root of all evil." But what a difference a few words make, for the truth of that verse is actually: "... The love of money is the root of all evil..."

Who sold the People of the Promise such a bogus bill of goods? Who told the poor that to make it to heaven they had to remain poor? My guess would be that lie was spawned in the pits of hell and propagated by the haves to ensure that the have-nots dare never aspire to be in the position of their oppressors.

To live a whole and prosperous life, it is imperative that each person realize that God desires His people to enjoy prosperity.

(3 John 1:2) **Beloved, I wish above all things that thou mayest prosper and be in health, even as thy soul prospereth.**

Even more, God actually takes great pleasure in the prosperity of his people:

(Psalms 35:27) **Let them shout for joy, and be glad, that favour my righteous cause: yea, let them say continually, Let the LORD be magnified, which hath pleasure in the prosperity of his servant.** (KJV)

Throughout the Bible, we find that those who have walked in relationship with, and served God, have enjoyed prosperity in their lives; and it only makes sense that we too, hope to be rewarded for our service to Him. Don't misunderstand, we should never enter into a relationship with God because we desire what he has, but rather, because we desire Him. The rewards are just added benefits.

(Matthew 6:27-33) **And which of you by being anxious can add one cubit to his span of life? And why are you anxious about** clothing? **Consider the lilies of the field, how they grow; they neither toil nor spin; yet I tell you, even Solomon in all his glory was not arrayed like one of these. But if God so clothes the grass of the field, which today is alive and tomorrow is thrown into the oven, will he not much more clothe you, O men of little faith? Therefore do not be anxious, saying, 'What shall we eat?' or 'What shall we drink?' or 'What shall we wear?' For the Gentiles seek all these things; and your heavenly Father knows that you need them all. But seek first his kingdom and his righteousness, and all these things shall be yours as well.** (RSV)

Realistically, who would volunteer to serve a great and awesome God that continually speaks of the blessings he has for those who love Him without hope that their life would be bettered in some way because of that relationship. Missionaries around the world understand that it is impossible to preach the gospel of a God that loves and cares without displaying that love and compassion of which they preach. In other words, it's difficult to preach the intangibles of God's kingdom, when hunger and other physical ailments are very real in their current lives. It's even more difficult for any person to believe in a God that can do all manner of great things in one's life when that God doesn't care enough to provide them with a decent meal.

Jesus realizing, that he had been sent here for a limited period of time (three and a half years)and that he had a lot of teaching to do, understood he needed to help as many people as possible physically before he could help them spiritually. More than any other thing during his earthly ministry, Jesus sought to break the curse of poverty and other circumstances surrounding the lives of those He came in contact with. While journeying through the countryside, he is continually found restoring sight to the blind, healing the lame and giving speech to those who could not speak. His passion for the disenfranchised was founded within His stated purpose for being on earth: **"I came that they might have life, and might have it abundantly"**.

Throughout His earthly ministry, Jesus went about healing and helping people. Because there were no social programs for those suffering from disabilities, other than the charity of friends, family and strangers with charitable hearts, Jesus produced food, healed sickness, and even occasionally resurrected from the dead.

Now, these people would no longer be "disadvantaged," but rather be on equal footing with their contemporaries, having the same opportunity to live a life that was rich both spiritually and physically. On one occasion Jesus resurrected a young man during a funeral procession. Why? Because his widowed mother was mourning beside him, and this woman would now have no one to help her economically. Jesus' miracle was as much an act of love for the boy as it was for the mother. He saved her from poverty. She might not be affluent, but at least she would be taken care of.

Referring back to the conversation with my friend, I wish that I had thought of defining "rich" from the start. To bring this point into even greater clarity, I should have expressed those thoughts to my friend in this manner, " I believe that everyone has the right to prosperity, which includes money, though not everyone will prosper."

As people of the promise, God makes all the abundance of this world available to us. We have the right to wealth and prosperity, however, many of us don't exercise those rights. What do I mean by rights? To understand rights we must first understand the concept of citizenship.

Because I am a citizen of the United States in good standing, there are certain rights and privileges that are granted me. For the purpose of this illustration, let's use the example of voting. I have the right to vote in elections that are pertinent to me as long as I do certain things. First, I must remain in good standing. There are certain laws that each citizen must abide by as a citizen of this country, to break them would render that person ineligible to partake of those rights and privileges. These same rules apply to the kingdom of God. As citizens of his kingdom, we must abide by his laws, or commandments, otherwise we become ineligible.

Realizing this next point might seem trivial, it cannot be emphasized enough. To enjoy the rights and privileges, you must know what they are. How can a citizen vote, if he or she is not aware of the election? Most people of promise don't enjoy the promises of God because they don't know what they are entitled to! If one has never been taught, or never taken the time to read and study the Word of God, it is safe to say there are many promises God has made that will never be realized.

Not long ago, I encountered some mechanical problems with my automobile while traveling. My first action was to call a family friend that lived in a nearby town to retrieve me and my belongings and return me safely to my home which was a considerable distance away. Secondly, I called the auto club of which I hold a membership, a form of citizenship that guarantees me certain privileges. After arranging for the tow, the person assisting me on the phone asked if I would need emergency overnight accommodations or a rental car to return home. Sadly, I had inconvenienced my friend to assist me at a late hour, when I had the means and resources at my disposal. Such is the case with citizenship in God's kingdom, we cannot utilize benefits that we don't know about.

Even sadder than those citizens who don't vote because they are unaware of elections, are those who know about the election, but choose not to exercise their right. On average, voter turnout across the nation has decreased significantly over the last several decades, while news outlets, media channels and other sources of information have increased significantly. Today, a vast majority of citizens forego their right to vote for whatever reason: be it apathy, a loss of faith in the government or the belief that their vote can't make a difference. Today, many of God's kingdom have a pessimistic outlook on their future and what it holds. Many have resolved themselves to the belief that they will forever be poor. And of course with that attitude, they will remain poor.

In every endeavor, there are universal laws that must be applied to succeed. No matter what you undertake, you must begin with a belief that you can and will succeed, develop and enact a plan for success, possess discipline to complete the necessary work, and then continue with the plan until successful. It's no wonder so many resolve to accept the crumbs that are left over, rather than dine at the buffet table of life. Every citizen of God's kingdom is eligible for wealth, but few will participate and even fewer will realize true prosperity.

I believe that all people have the right to be prosperous, if we only search for God's blessings and adhere to his instructions. But, if you seek "true" prosperity, there is one thing that will make you feel richer than anything else… that's inner peace. Peace is perhaps the greatest blessing from God, and it will be the topic of the final chapter.

(1 Chronicles 29:12) **Riches and honor come from you, and you rule over all. In your hand are power and might; and it is in your hand to make great and to give strength to all.** (NRSV)

(Deuteronomy 8:18) **But remember the LORD your God, for it is he who gives you power to get wealth, so that he may confirm his covenant that he swore to your ancestors, as he is doing today.** (NRSV)

23

PEACE IS ALWAYS PRESENT WITHIN THE PROMISE

(Genesis 21:22) **And it happened at that time, Abimelech and Phicol, the commander of his army, spoke to Abraham, saying, God is with you in all that you do.** (MKJV)

(Genesis 24:1) **Now Abraham was old, advanced in age; and the LORD had blessed Abraham in every way.** (NASB)

Peace comes from within. Do not seek it without. -Buddha

Each one has to find his peace from within. And peace to be real must be unaffected by outside circumstances .-Mohandas Gandhi

Where ignorance is our master, there is no possibility of real peace. –the Dalai Lama

The greatest source of confusion and discouragement to the people of promise happens when they encounter troubles along their journey. Unfortunately, most promise seekers are not prepared to handle these disappointments. Most are surprised to experience obstacles because they foolishly believed that faith in God would assure them a life of ease. Actually, the exact opposite is more truthful; a belief in God does not guarantee a life without challenges. This erroneous belief has resulted in many of past centuries deserting the course, and will cause many of future generations to abandon the walk as well. The truth of the matter is, for all people, believers and non-believers alike, problems are par for the course and hardships will hit us all. Yes, believers are bound to carry their share of burdens.

To say that the greatest benefit of the Promise is a life of peace might seem contradictory after the opening paragraph, but it is the utmost truth: Peace is always present within the Promise. How is it, then, that peace and problems can coexist within one's life?

If there is a contradiction, its' source is rooted in one's comprehension of peace. Peace does not mean the absence of problems in one's life, but rather, the absence of the panic and dread that results when those problems are encountered. In other words, the problems are present but the fear is not.

Throughout Abraham's life we find that he continually overcomes obstacles that stand between him and the promise given by God. His life was far from easy, as surely you feel yours is. The secret for his tenacity is a secret we have much to learn from:

(Genesis 22:1-8) **After these things God tested Abraham. He said to him, "Abraham!" And he said, "Here I am." He said, "Take your son, your only son Isaac, whom you love, and go to the land of Moriah, and offer him there as a burnt offering on one of the mountains that I shall show you." So Abraham rose early in the morning, saddled his donkey, and took two of his young men with him, and his son Isaac; he cut the wood for the burnt offering, and set out and went to the place in the distance** that God had shown him. On the third day Abraham looked up and saw the place far away. Then Abraham said to his young men, "Stay here with the donkey; the boy and I will go over there; we will worship, and then we will come back to you." Abraham took the wood of the burnt offering and laid it on his son Isaac, and he himself carried the fire and the knife. So the two of them walked on together. Isaac said to his father Abraham, "Father!" And he said, "Here I am, my son." He said, "The fire and the wood are here, but where is the lamb for a burnt offering?" Abraham said, "God himself will provide the lamb for a burnt offering, my son. " So the two of them walked on together. (NRSV)

Talk about a crisis of faith! How could God, the One who gave the promise, now totally reverse course, and ask him to murder the object of the promise? How could he ask this? After all, Abraham bore the promise through foreign lands and various hardships for more than twenty-five years. Through it all he believed when every circumstance said it would not happen. Now, he is called to end the life of the child he didn't ask for but had grown to love. And just as he had begun his journey to the fulfillment of the promise with nothing more than a word of instruction, he was called to end it all with nothing more than a word of instruction.

To make matters worse, it even seems as if God taunts Abraham to make an impossible decision even harder. In Verse 2, the angel says to Abraham, "Take your son, your only son, whom you love". Then God gives Abraham more time to think about his sacrifice; instead of allowing him to do it quickly, Abraham must travel three full days just to get to the general region and then walk a good distance to arrive at the actual site of sacrifice. God allowed Abraham plenty of time to think about the sacrifice he would have to make.

Imagine what thoughts must have weighed heavy on Abraham's heart as he and his son traveled together. Would you describe a man in such a situation at peace, with peaceful thoughts, free from worry? Of course not. Likely his thoughts were more like a wave in a storm, fighting against him with brute force. Did Abraham's faith ever waver, even as he climbed the mountain terrain, or as he built the altar and placed his son there? If so, the bible doesn't say. What he do know is he was obedient to the letter.

Then, just as Abraham raised the knife to kill his only son, the Lord called out to him to stop in Verse 11. In Verse 12, God reveals to Abraham the reason for such an excruciating test, "for now I know that you fear God since you would not withhold your only son from me." Although the fear in Verse 12 refers to a reverence of God by Abraham, this reverence was one based in love and respect for the power of God rather than fear from retribution of God. Because Abraham believed that anything God asked him to do would work out for his good in the end, he was able to do what most men would have failed to begin, much less complete.

Abraham was a man of extraordinary faith because he realized succeeding at his call did not require him to understand, or even to believe what God said, but, he must only trust and complete what God said. This revelation was Abraham's basis for peace, and should be our source of stability amongst all of our trials.

(Romans 8:28) **And we know that God causes all things to work together for good to those who love God, to those who are called according to His purpose.** (NAS95)

In Genesis 12, when God promised Abraham, "I will bless them that bless you, and I will curse them that curse you." God, by saying "I will," actually relieves Abraham of the performance anxiety surrounding his promise. God, in effect, assures Abraham that as long as he walked in the promise he had been given, he [God] assumed responsibility for the outcome. It was not Abraham's responsibility to bring forth a son, consequently, it was not Abraham's responsibility to ensure that his son became a nation. Abraham was off the hook! Can you imagine how liberating that must be?

That same peace Abraham enjoyed can be yours, because just as God promised Abraham "I will", he has promised the same to you. Actually, this concept of peace has been enjoyed by many great biblical figures who understood God was in control and he could be trusted to take care of his children. The pages of the Bible are littered with many who understood that the "peace" of God required total trust, and these people of promise made bold and daring declarations to the goodness and the faithfulness of God. One of the most encouraging examples, one that might put you in mind of

Abraham, is found in 2 Kings chapter 4. Here a woman, who had no children, was promised by the prophet Elisha, that God would bless her with a child. Although the woman revered the anointing of God's prophet—this was proven by her insistence to provide guest quarters for the traveling evangelist to use whenever he was in town-- this promise must have stretched her faith because the text states that she was "barren" and "her husband was old." Nonetheless, she believed the Word from the prophet and in due time she bore a child as promised.

And, as is typical, the wait for the manifestation of the promise; her child's birth, was not the end of her promise, or her problems. Rather, it was the start of a new phase within her promise, because after the child had grown, he became sick one morning while harvesting the crops with his father. After one of the workers had taken the child back to his mother, he died after resting on her lap until noon. Once again, the object of the promise was jeopardized, and the promise bearer would have to trust God or give in to the fear of the situation.

In the ensuing moments of her loss, this woman who had just experienced great loss displays how to rest in the peace of God, when life is full of trouble. The woman immediately sent to her husband for one of the young male workers to bring a donkey for her to ride in pursuit of God's prophet. When questioned by her husband as to why she must go and the condition of their child, she simply replies "It is well." To understand how profound her statement was, it is necessary to translate the word "well" back to its' original Hebrew form, which is "shalom" or "peace". In other words, the woman refused to speak about the situation in terms of the apparent problem, but chose rather to address it in terms of her God-given promise by declaring "It is well", meaning, "my soul is at peace because my child shall live!!"

The word shalom, although defined as peace, implies so much more. Most, if not all of the great Bible heroes have endured challenges while pursuing their Promise before recognizing and appreciating the shalom of God in varying forms.

The wisdom writers of Proverbs understood the shalom of God increases both the quality and quantity of life:

(Proverbs 3:1-2) **My son, forget not my law; but let thine heart keep my commandments: For length of days, and long life, and peace [shalom], shall they add to thee.** (KJV)

Those writers also understood its' value and how to attain it:

(Proverbs 3:13-17) **Happy is the man that findeth wisdom, and the man that getteth understanding. For the merchandise of it is better than the merchandise of silver, and the gain thereof than fine gold. She is more precious than rubies: and all the things thou canst desire are not to be compared unto her. Length of days is in her right hand; and in her left hand riches and honour. Her ways are ways of pleasantness, and all her paths are peace [shalom].** (KJV)

However, when we examine the use of the word shalom as it applied to the way God blessed various biblical heroes when facing diverse trials, it becomes evident that the Peace of the Promise is universal to all situations and all in need. David, Solomon, Job, and many others, understood the shalom of God to be:

Safety

(Job 21:9) **Their houses are safe<shalom> from fear, neither is the rod of God upon them.** (KJV)

Peace

(Psalms 4:8) **I will both lay me down in peace<shalom>, and sleep: for thou, LORD, only makest me dwell in safety.** (KJV)

Prosperity

(Psalms 35:27) **Let them shout for joy, and be glad, that favor my righteous cause: Yea, let them say continually, Jehovah be magnified, Who hath pleasure in the prosperity<shalom> of his servant.** (ASV)

Happiness

(Psalms 37:11) **But the meek shall inherit the earth; and shall delight themselves in the abundance of peace<shalom>.** (KJV)

Now, you understand that the Peace of God means so much more. It actually refers to a wholeness or completeness of life. To be whole, means there is nothing missing or lost. The peace that is derived from the promise is that type of whole- life peace, a life that is balanced and suffers no inadequacies-- a life that is blessed in all areas.

To enjoy the Peace of the Promise is to rest in God's ability to do everything He has promised. To say that one has the PEACE of God is not to say, that situations and circumstances will not arise bringing stress, duress and heartache to God's people. It is to say, that those who fully believe and stand on those promises, wholly understand that in the end God has our well being firmly secured.

Today, the new generation of People of Promise must begin to share the many great victories God continues to orchestrate on behalf of his people.

Consider the case of Susan, a person of great faith, who almost forgot that God was on her side. Susan, a loyal and dedicated employee had worked for a medical supply company for several years, ascending the corporate ladder to the rank of regional manager. Although she was quite capable; her teams always scored at or near the top in company-wide sales competitions, Susan had already seen others who were less capable promoted instead of her. She began to feel that she had reached the glass ceiling within her company and further advancement seemed out of the question.

When news spread that a senior level officer would be leaving the company, it was widely believed that one of the vice-president positions would soon be vacant. Although she tried not to become excited, Susan couldn't help but think, "God, I've paid my dues, and I really want this position…God please."

When one of Susan's colleagues, a person with a less stellar record of performance, less seniority and a past marred by several questionable and not-so-secret management decisions was chosen, Susan lost heart. So much so that she not only thought about quitting her job, she almost quit her faith. "Eventually, after a few weeks of heartbreak, I came to my senses, and climbed back on the horse," she said, "But I still questioned God as to why I wasn't the one chosen."

The next year was a challenging year for Susan. Many of her family members lost their jobs due to a tough economic climate; Susan was called on and gladly helped. Her father was diagnosed with cancer, and Susan encountered some health challenges as well. But through it all, Susan was able to maintain a positive attitude and had a good year at work.

Near the end of that fiscal year, the company grapevine buzzed with news that the company would undergo a major downsizing in the very near future. Susan, like everyone else, waited on pins and needles. She thought, "God I need my job, not just for me, but for my family as well. Please God, don't let me down." She added, "As I prayed, I tried not to think about how disappointed I was when God didn't come through with the promotion. I tried to focus on the matters at hand, just keeping my job."

When the official announcement was made Susan was overjoyed to find out that God had been at work answering her prayers, long before she prayed them. It turned out that the company was laying off an entire business division, every position from top to bottom. Amazingly for Susan, it was the division that she had hoped to head less than a year ago. "I felt overjoyed and ashamed all at the same time. I was overjoyed because now I could see that God did not allow me to get that job, because I would have been out of a job in less than a year. But, at the same time, I was ashamed because I had doubted God. I had to be reminded that Romans 8:28 is true, 'all things do work together for the good of those that love God and are called according to his purpose'. Now I don't question why things do or don't happen, I just trust that God has his reason for whatever happens. One thing is for sure, he knows better what I need than I do." Susan has learned to trust God and rest in the shalom of his promises.

Bud also learned that sometimes, God's desire for our well-being requires painful interjections, before his peace can be experienced. One Saturday morning he and several riding buddies from church set out on a scenic motorcycle ride through the Texas Hill Country, just outside of Austin. A little while into the ride, one of the riders drove off of the roadway. As panic ensued during the moments after, Bud chose to stand on the promises of God to heal those who believed. During those moments Bud reminded God of His Promises in His Word regarding healing. He reminded God that when believers lay hands the sick are to recover. He quoted Isaiah 53:5 declaring , "Jesus was wounded for our transgressions, he was bruised for our iniquities: the chastisement of our peace was upon him; and with his stripes we are healed." He even called upon the angels of God to heal his friend.

As the group of riders waited for the ambulance to arrive, Bud remained in faith that his friend would get up and walk away from the accident scene. It wasn't until the ambulance pulled away with the injured rider strapped to a stretcher that Bud allowed any thought of God not answering his prayers to enter his mind. "All that day, I questioned God about why my friend didn't get up and walk away from the accident. It wasn't until sometime later, that I felt as if God was saying that he didn't get up so that a greater good could be served. I didn't understand what that meant, but I felt strongly that's what the Spirit was saying."

That greater good was served. It turned out that Bud's friend had an advanced case of cancer. Had he not been rushed to the hospital and subjected to a barrage of tests, the cancer might not have been detected until it was too late. This experience taught Bud that sometimes the ultimate peace of God requires some painful moments.

Just like Susan, Bud and our predecessors in faith, we must trust that no matter what happens, God will work on our behalf to make it all good in the end.

It is God's ultimate desire that each of his people take hold of their promises and live a fulfilling life anchored in his promises. The dictionary defines peace as freedom from disquieting or oppressive thoughts or emotions. That peace is found when you ignore the false information of your circumstances and focus on the realities of your God-given promises. That ultimate peace can only be found when you trust God to do all that he promised. You must let go and let God do what only God can, and will do.

Finally, we belong to God, from this life and beyond through eternity. God's promises guarantee our fulfillment here on earth if we merely act out of faith. But God also desires for us to make it to our final land of promise with him. For this reason, he will never leave us without promises. After we have found our promises in the earthly realm, we will begin our journey to another land of promise. The apostle Paul offers the best advice for both our earthly and our final spiritual journey:

And the peace of God, which passeth all understanding, shall keep your hearts and minds through Christ Jesus. (Philippians 4:7 KJV)

I hope all the things we've seen in this book, all the scriptures and all the encouragement, will help you to stay on the right course, the course of God's promises, the course that keeps you—and all of us—close to God, a closeness preserved for God's friends, like Abraham was, like you can be.

Please remember that there will be problems, difficulties and disappointments that will work to discourage you. Through all the scriptures, whose life was perfect? Who lived without any problems? Not one soul of all the people of promise live *perfect* lives, but you can live the *promised* life. You are promised a life of purpose to guide you; A life of passion to inspire you; A life of power that makes all things possible; A life of prosperity to reward you; and a life that is pleasurable through peace.

Keep your faith, and keep holding to God's promises, and you will find the peace of God that surpasses any other feeling or thought, a peace that can only be found with help from our Creator. Take these final scriptures to mind as you pursue the promises of God, and may the peace of God find you as you find an abundance of love, happiness, and prosperity to fill your heart forever... Now this is the your ultimate life!

Peace I leave with you, my peace I give unto you: not as the world giveth, give I unto you. Let not your heart be troubled, neither let it be afraid. (John 14:27 KJV)

These things I have spoken unto you, that in me ye might have peace. In the world ye shall have tribulation: but be of good cheer; I have overcome the world. (John 16:33 KJV)

ABOUT THE AUTHOR

BYRON RAVNELL is a spiritual leader and motivational speaker who coaches and empowers people from all walks of life to live powerful, effective and whole lives through practical application of Scripture and spiritual truths.

A gifted communicator, Byron's ability to reach, teach and entertain was developed through many years as an on-air radio personality for several radio stations. His ability to take difficult spiritual concepts and make them easily understandable through simple teachings and life applications has allowed him to aid many uncover the fullness that a true life of promise offers.

An entrepreneur from his youth, Byron started his first business at age 15, allowing tremendous opportunities to encounter, and experience people from every conceivable background in various settings; these skills, along with a love for the things of God as well as the people of God, have crafted Byron's authentic and unique voice for the spiritual wilderness of today to assist those in search of an abundant life.

For more information or speaking engagements, visit **www.byronravnell.com**.

www.ingramcontent.com/pod-product-compliance
Lightning Source LLC
LaVergne TN
LVHW051638080426
835511LV00016B/2381